everything living has a higher purpose. Its goal is to bring God back into art in a nonreligious manner and thus ignite enthusiasm like the action of divine madness.

At the same time, Stuckism preserves certain postmodern impulses. its most striking postmodern feature is its relationship to "-isms," which it casts doubt upon for being too-narrow definitions of artistic flow. At the same time, it also put an "-ism" into its own name in order to make it clear that it is both modernist and postmodernist, but at the same time neither one nor the other. Stuckism is considered an international "non-movement" that is spontaneous and doesn't create any structures (a postmodernist feature), but at the same time it does have the character of a movement with its "-ism" (a modernist feature). Another postmodernist feature of Stuckism is that painting operates for it as a process whose actual goal isn't the creation of a work of art with its immanent qualities, but spiritual self-knowledge and the rebirth of society. Stuckism, like postmodernism, understands works of art as an element of a certain broader process or context, and in their case, the process and context are spiritual. The rapid spread of Stuckism to many countries around the world, and the emergence of an international movement that also includes sculptors and graphic artists testifies to a change in artistic sensibility. In the beginning, there were thirteen artists who professed Stuckism, but today there are two hundred thirty-six Stuckist groups in fifty-two countries.[73]

In 2016 the "Manifesto of Radical Realism" was published in Prague by its authors, the Czech and Russian artists and theorists Vasil Artamonov, Dominik Forman, Michael Hauser, Alexey Klyuykov, and Avdey Ter-Oganyan. This manifesto first presents a critique of the present state of art, which could bring the thesis of the "Stuckist Manifesto" to mind. According to the radical realists, contemporary art is in agony. It is dominated by postconceptualist installations and projects that parasitize various non-artistic fields of activity, such as the natural sciences, sociology, and political activism. The Manifesto rejects the postmodern patterns that foreground institutional, cultural, and social contexts of art, while pushing the work itself to the margins and depleting its significance. "Paintings, statues, videos, and objects are mere pieces in the jigsaw puzzle of artists-managers or artists-curators. The context of these jigsaw puzzles holds all the meaning: the work itself is in the last place." However, radical realism is fundamentally different from Stuckism in its focus. The radical realists oppose art that invokes the authenticity of individual experience, originality, or spiritual depths because it's made by artists whose individualism and originality are prefabricated and harmonize with the logic of contemporary late capitalism.

They create a kind of pseudo-works that look like "miserable caricatures of the old masters of the premodern eras" or that are the result of mixing "modernist morphology with postmodern principles." In this point, one can find criticism not only of postmodernism but also of Stuckism, which understands the work of art as a medium for expressing authentic spiritual experiences. Radical realism does the exact opposite of what Stuckism is aiming at. The medium of painting, sculpture, or another art genre should be the bearer of autonomous artistic forms. The work is no longer a means for expressing "authentic" experiences, but rather it's a site where immanent artistic qualities, including composition and morphology crystallize. The work again becomes the meaning of artistic activity. The autonomy of the work is understood in radical realism to be in a dialectical relationship with social reality. In the sense of Lukács's and Lifšic's aesthetic theory the work of art is autonomous in that it has a distance from immediate psychological states, social contexts, and political practices, and thanks to this distance it is able to capture their paradigmatic or characteristic features and tendencies in a concrete way. Instead of the Stuckist connection to the spiritual dimension of reality, radical realist artistic activity is connected with contents that "reproduce the contradictions and crises of today and at the same time express advances toward a post-capitalist society." Radical realism is remarkable for creating a specific relationship to the political dimension in the sense of elements of the communist idea in their past forms as well as their hypothetical future incarnation. This political dimension allows art to create a free space outside of the thinking, perceiving, and practices in an art world permeated by the logic of late capitalism, and in order to gain distance from the demands, ideas, and the real state of contemporary art and society. The political dimension of radical realism is no longer merely "alternative," but is named as communist. The Manifesto states that this political dimension is a condition of the renewal of art as the "artistic recreation of the human being, form, and perspective, precisely in the spectral emptiness of today's art."[74] Radical realism follows the art forms that preceded modernism, but these are artists of a different type than Kandinsky and the other "spiritual" modernists endorsed by Stuckism. They are mainly artists from the Soviet era who developed the "raw" style; for example, Nikolai Andronov, Viktor Popkov, Andrei Vasnetsov, and Geliy Korzhev. These artists incorporated certain impulses from modernism and the avant-garde into realistic art and continued in the realist tradition in a creative manner even in a period when pop art, conceptualism, and other postmodern trends began to dominate in the West. The radical realists evaluate Stuckism as a significant but historically obsolete act. In Dominik Forman's words: "The

Stuckists have already fulfilled their purpose, painting has been accepted as a medium for a long time. We have to go further and decide what a truly noble, truthful, and socialist painting (or perhaps another type of art—it doesn't have to be painting) should look. The kind that truly affects both the educated and the uneducated viewer, whose form will express content that has the goal of being a single, comprehensible, affecting and truthful work. The Stuckists did not fulfill their goal expressed in words—the form absolutely does not correspond to the intended content. We are continually struggling with something similar, but at least we are already aware of the problem."[75]

Stuckism and radical realism are examples of artistic trends that oppose the postmodernist patterns—contextuality, deconstruction of the work of art, and the "end of art"—that had become institutionalized artistic approaches and a kind of orthodoxy that feigned subversion of all orthodoxies. Patterns appear in these trends that act like a return and renewal of modernist or even classical artistic approaches, but in their recreation we find elements of postmodernist patterns. In Stuckism it's a refusal to define any binding principles for creating art that would make Stuckism into a modernist "'ism." In radical realism it's the initial approach to painting, sculpture, film, video, and other types of art as "media" that have the same value and cannot be divided into higher and lower genres. Connecting with a particular medium is a matter of choice, which is essentially random (given by certain circumstances and individual factors), and isn't necessarily a result of the qualitative preference for a particular medium as such. In this point, radical realism takes postmodernist intermediality as a point of departure, even though it disagrees with its institutionalized form. The pattern of intermediality assumes that there is a multiplicity of equally valuable media that can be interlinked without compromising the artistic value of one particular medium. For example, the connection of painting and video installations doesn't diminish the value of the genre of painting. The radical realists reverse the direction of artistic activity and instead of the postmodernist links between individual media, they focus on the inner possibilities of a particular medium, which doesn't have to necessarily be painting but in principle could be any artistic genre. They do this because intermedialism along with other postmodernist patterns gradually led to the emptying of the artistic genres themselves, which effectively disrupted intermedialism as an established artistic approach because it had become a way to connect things that no longer existed. Alexey Klyuykov expressed it like this: ". . . we are not addressing the dominance of one media over another. We're addressing consistent work with a chosen medium. In the Manifesto of Radical Realism the word painting wasn't used at all (but despite that, everyone read it as a manifesto proclaiming painting 'über alles'). Yes, we've chosen painting for several reasons, and we work in this medium. It could have been film, it could have been sculpture, but we didn't have sufficient training. At the same time, pictures seem to be very comprehensible for viewers."[76]

Despite all the fundamental differences between Stuckism and radical realism, we find postmodernist patterns in them, such as rejection of a binding definition for the trend (Stuckism) and the assumption of the same value across artistic media (radical realism). However, these patterns are in relationship with modernist or even classical artistic principles and approaches such as the "spiritual dimension of art" (Stuckism) or the autonomy of the work of art, form-creating realism, the discipline of artistic work and following historical masters (radical realism). The postmodernist patterns are neither dominant nor at the core, nor are they entirely displaced. Here, artistic creation is similar to a circulation among postmodernist, modernist, and even classical principles, which prevents these artistic trends from being a simple return to historical modernism or to classical art.

The Domain of Cultural Theory: Fiduciary Realism, Monism, and the Affective Turn

In connection with these artistic tendencies, or independently of them, theoretical conceptions arise that aim to capture the more general character of these new phenomena after the end of postmodernism. Cultural theories are appearing that differ from the postmodern theories we know from Lyotard, Baudrillard, and others. In this sense, David Rudrum draws attention to the difference between Lyotard and Bourriaud as an arti theorist of the new generation. Lyotard was attracted to investigating the boundaries of representation and he thought of a dimension that lies outside the realm of the representable. Bourriaud raises the question of community and the recreation of social ties and new social forms associated with "everyday micro-utopias" appear.[77]

Ihab Hassan, who is one of the most prominent contemporary postmodern literary theorists, writes that multiplicity, plurality, and diversity have led to tribalism, fundamentalism, a fragmentation of micronarratives and the abandonment of a sense for truth, the public sphere, and planetary citizenship.[78] He encourages the restoration of what fell apart due to the influence of postmodernism and its mutations. Truth, the public sphere, social reality, realism, and planetary citizenship are typologically classified as modernist concepts. Hassan did not thematize these concepts in his books from the postmodern period. They formed the political horizon and the unspoken peripheral patterns of his literary theory, similarly as had been the case with Derrida, Lyotard, and other postmodern thinkers. Hassan is reacting to the mutation of postmodernist patterns that took place after the extinction of the egalitarian civic political horizon and the modernist peripheral patterns.

This cultural theorist recognized that postmodernism had mutated, even though he doesn't use the term mutation. He then encourages the renewal of the best parts of the spirit of modernism. In my terminology, he endeavors to renew the postmodernist patterns as they were before the mutations took place. He proposes to create a postmodern or fiduciary realism that is based on Nothingness as the basis for representing reality. Nothingness is an expression for "undoing" our knowledge; that is, for the conscious suspension of our knowledge and its loosening or disintegration. Hassan conceives of this act as a kenosis of the subject, a concept derived from Christian theology. In his view, kenosis as an emptiness or depletion of his own ego expresses a postmodern spiritual position that allows him to restore confidence, faith, and empathy for reality. Hassan, like the Stuckists, is turning to a spiritual experience of reality. In the finite world, flashes of the infinite and immersion into Nothingness can be seen, and kenosis renews the original relations between the human being and the world, which are in harmony with the needs of the planet and of geopolitics. Fiduciary realism thus contains elements of postmodernism, modernism, and premodernism. We can understand this complex of ideas and values as a renewal of "the best from postmodernism," in which postmodernism is actually deepened or radicalized through the theological concept of kenosis in connection with the discovery of Nothingness as the last basis of postmodernism.[79]

Other concepts also appear in cultural theory that capture this desire to renew the relationship with reality in contemporary art. Jameson argues that one of the main features of postmodern culture was the disjunction of the signifier from the signified, which is associated with the loosening or diffusion of any definable "meaning," that is, the signified, and with the obscuring of the referent and of reality itself.[80] In his concept of performativism, Raoul Eshelman declares that in contemporary literature, for example in Yann Martel's novel *The Life of Pi*, this dualistic division of signifier and signifies disappears and a tendency connect them, which he calls monism, appears. He associates this tendency with a change in the character of the literary text, in which the factors of semantic unification and hierarchization and delimitation are strengthened without abandoning the postmodern multiplicity of perspectives.[81] The literary text and the authorial subject are the result of a multiplicity of overlapping semantic frames, which cannot be transferred to a single core. However, these frames are not made up of floating signifiers, because they are anchored in social interactions which take place in the physical reality of human beings.[82]

Another feature of postmodern culture was the disappearance of emotion and depth, which Jameson says is illustrated by Warhol's depiction of human figures (e.g., Marilyn Monroe) as commodified objects.[83] Contemporary cultural theorists (Massumi, Grossberg, Berlant) point out that an "affective turn" is taking place in a variety of artistic genres. Affects are conceived as "non-cognitive and non-representational intensities that take place outside of consciousness," whereas emotions "emerge when such intensities are narrativised, named and represented as part of individual experience" (Pieter Vermeulen).[84] In his analysis of postirony, Lee Konstantinou writes about Jeffrey Eugenides's novel *The Marriage Plot*, in which the student Madeleine attends a course on semiotics where she is acquainted with Barthes's *A Lovers Discourse: Fragments* and entertains the idea that one should get rid of the tyranny of love upon realizing that love is a cultural construct and its symptoms are purely mental. But then Madeleine rejects this idea, because love is something different. "She could read Barthes' deconstructions of love all day without feeling her love for Leonard diminish the teeniest little bit."[85] In this novel, love manifests itself as an affect that isn't a cultural construct and it can't be transferred to a moving sign. Love is an ironization of deconstruction. However, according to Konstantinou, the contemporary "metamodernist" nature of love doesn't correspond to the way it was grasped artistically or theoretically in earlier periods. In contemporary literature, this affect is no longer perceived as a binding and tyrannizing construction, as it had been in modernism, but he also doesn't see a return of the previous forms of love in it. The current depiction of love in literature is neither postmodern nor modern, but at the same time there are elements of both in it.

Fiduciary realism (Hassan), monism (Eshelman) and the metamodernist conception of affect (Konstantinou) can be interpreted as working with the "spirit of postmodernism," as Ihab Hassan would express it. However, he requires movement in a different direction than ironization, floating signifiers or a multiplicity of perspectives. It seems as if the spirit of postmodernism can only be saved by turning in the opposite direction and connecting with modernist seriousness, a "monism" of the signifier and signified, and with a viewpoint of reality. We find that in these concepts, generally speaking, there are circulations between an effort at renewing the original meaning of postmodernism and awareness that it is only possible to do this by abandoning the postmodernist patterns whose development led to an empty nihilism. These are circulations between the spirit of postmodernism and the desire to restore the principles of modernism or egalitarian citizenship which, as Hassan writes, postmodernism had helped to weaken and deplete. It's a circulation that is taking place around these two crystallized focal points with no way to determine which of the two is dominant.

The Domain of Theology: Radical Orthodoxy

For several authors and trends after the end of postmodernism we have noted that their response to postmodernism and its mutations is a revival of spirituality in the form of a spiritual experience of reality in which premodern intellectual and artistic sources open up (Stuckism, remodernism, Hassan, Eshelman). The first trend that reacted in this spiritual way to postmodernism was radical orthodoxy. Its theological responses display the same kind of ambiguous relationship to postmodernism that was seen in trends and concepts after 2000. However, radical orthodoxy went much farther in its response than the other trends. Its representatives elaborated not only a critique of postmodernism and modernism but also of their own politics, ethics, and ontology. John Milbank and other representatives of radical orthodoxy understand postmodern philosophy and culture as a radicalization and culmination of the decadence and nihilism whose intellectual preconditions arose in the Middle Ages in Duns Scotus's theology. This theologian had formulated the conception of the univocity of being, which Millbank argues became the root of the later division of reason and revelation, philosophy and theology, and Christianity and the state, as a result of which modern and postmodern philosophy and the modern state lost their source of spiritual values and fell into nihilism. At the same time, however, radical orthodoxy also believes that postmodern thinking has never successfully fulfilled its own intentions. These unfulfilled intentions of postmodernism are the multiple and related understanding of reality, difference, non-hierarchism, and participation. From the perspective of radical orthodoxy, these postmodern patterns were not fulfilled because they lacked a "grand narrative," which is Christian participatory metaphysics, as we find in St. Augustine, St. Thomas Aquinas, and the patristic theologians. In this metaphysics, the bond between God and Creation has not yet been broken, and dualities (reason/revelation, etc.) containing the germs of the nihilism of values had not yet appeared. Radical orthodoxy follows this "premodern" metaphysics, but its own conceptions are premodern only in certain aspects. They are premodern in the sense that Milbank and the other leaders attempt to renew a metaphysics in which there isn't a dualistic gap between Creation and God, but a relationship of participation. However, it is not premodern, because it doesn't understand reality as a pregiven order created through a hierarchy of genera, species, substances, and accidents. Radical orthodoxy draws on Derrida, Lyotard, and Deleuze. Its basic concepts are the multiplicity of differences and the movement of differentiation, nonbinary thinking, and deconstruction of the metaphysics of violence, in which the unity and the whole mean suppressing the individuality and the particularity of the unified elements. These postmodern concepts and approaches are an intellectual foundation for creating a radically orthodox "ontology of peace," in which relations among individual entities aren't based on strife and rivalry. This ontology is supposed to be a fulfillment of the intentions of postmodernism that are expressed in deconstruction and the critique of the metaphysics of violence. However, according to radical orthodox thinkers, postmodern philosophy cannot fulfill its own intentions, because it has a hidden basis: the ontology of strife and struggle. This is evident, for example, in Lyotard's concept of the "differend" (*le différend*), which means "difference," but in the same sense as "dispute." This theory arose out of the assumption that each unifying "discursive genre" necessarily distorts the meaning of individual instances of speech. As a result, there is an unavoidable conflict situation between individual speeches because there is no unifying discourse that would prevent this situation from arising. Therefore, Milbank argues that postmodern philosophy is tied to an ontology that gives rise to conflict situations. This "ontology of violence" means that the intentions of Lyotard's or Derrida's philosophy, which consist in a critique of violence, cannot be fulfilled. Milbank then seeks to fulfill the intentions of postmodernism by transferring the concepts of multiplicity, difference, and non-hierarchism to a different ontological basis, which is the basis provided by Christianity in the form of its "orthodox" theology according to St. Augustine and St. Thomas Aquinas. In Milbank's interpretation, the principles and concepts of Christianity are not in contradiction with postmodern conceptions; on the contrary, they provide a starting point for fulfilling postmodernism's intentions. Milbank creates a "radical" interpretation of Christianity, and claims that Christianity differs from other religions or political ideologies because it can become "internally" postmodern. Although Christianity has not resisted the temptation to become a totalizing system in its history, its central concepts disrupt the metaphysical ideas about immutable essences in humankind, society, and the cosmos. The created world arose from nothing, is related to the eternal, and can be interpreted as an insubstantial reality that is composed from the continuous flow of relational differences.[86] Judaism and Islam are religions that are too monotheist, and evoke the idea of God as an indivisible absolute. Neither of them allows us to conceive of God as a process of difference, and Millbank says this is why we cannot interpret them in a postmodern manner. By contrast, polytheisms, as religions of multiplicity would seem to be in accordance with the postmodern idea of radical plurality, but this multiplicity has led to discord and power struggles between contending gods, such as in the Titanomachy. This created the need for a unifying deity to quell the conflicts within polytheism. For Milbank, it's therefore clear that the intentions of postmodernism cannot be fulfilled either by the strict monotheism of Islam and Judaism or by a pluralist polytheism. He therefore takes Christianity with its trinitarian conception of God as his starting point. Within this theological figure there transpires a process of differentiation of the meaning of the divine persons in relation to human history, in which the Son is incarnated into as the second divine person, and the Holy Spirit acts within it as the principle of the Christian community. The Christian conception of God can be interpreted in such a way that God is the symbol of differentiation. However, it does not lead to the disintegration of God into a disconnected multiplicity of individual persons, because it is a differentiation connected with the creation of the insubstantial unity based on a relationship of love among the individual persons. More and more differences arise between people, which creates their "infinite relationship" that corresponds to Derrida's concept of differentiation, but with the difference that a nonviolent principle of unity, expressed as the relationship of love between the divine persons is active here.[87] We can approach Milbank's interpretation of the Trinity using an example from the history of music. The difference between the persons in the Trinity develop in a way reminiscent of Renaissance polyphony, which relies on individually conducted voices, which at a given movement in the composition's development can be in disharmony with the others. Individual voices create harmony that isn't based on a fundamental harmonic pattern (the essence of the composition), but on a process of the composition's development. Milbank argues that the Christian conception of God as a Trinity demonstrates that Christianity is, firstly, compatible with postmodernism (and therefore should be afforded preference over other religions), and, secondly, that it offers a pattern of a nonviolent and insubstantial process of unification. This pattern is the basis of the ontology of peace, which enables the fulfillment of postmodernism's intentions.

In other words, Milbank is confirming that postmodernism has a prosthetic character, because he believes its way of developing postmodern patterns (plurality and difference) is dependent upon a particular ontology in the background. However, he overlooks the fact that early postmodernism had a radically emancipatory horizon that lent a different tone to this strife and rivalry that he himself describes as an ontology of violence with a nihilist flavor. In my view, this ontology is the result of the extinction of the emancipatory peripheral patterns connected with the traces of the communist idea. Milbank thus mistakenly assumes that a nihilistic ontology has been part of postmodernism since its beginnings, when it is actually the result of the radically emancipatory horizon that originally belonged to postmodernism.

Radical orthodoxy arose as a circulation between the postmodern patterns of differentiation, antiessentialism, and premodernist conceptions of the Trinitarian God, and participation of Creation in divine being. What is remarkable is that these circulations are conceived as the fulfillment of postmodernism's intentions. However, I understand the premodernist patterns mentioned above as a substitute for the extinguished traces of the communist idea that were supposed to be the condition for the possibility and impossibility of fulfilling the postmodernist vision of nonviolent social relations that respect the uniqueness of each person.

The Domain of Politics: The Identitarian Movement, the Islamic State, and Metapopulism

We can supplement the list of formations that emerge in the domain of art, cultural theory, philosophy, and theology with phenomena that are appearing in political thinking and political life. We have already examined the Identitarian movement and de Benoist's political philosophy, in which there is a radically conservative or neofascist mutation of postmodernism. In this political and intellectual trend, a vision of cultural identity arises in which the postmodern patterns of difference, multiplicity, and the critique of universalism are connected with purified cultural and ethnic values that are supposed to save Europe and other civilizations from a nihilistic plague of mixed values.

Jörg Heiser describes yet another example of a political phenomenon that consists in a hybrid or "superhybrid" connection of postmodernist and premodernist patterns: the Islamic State and its propaganda videos. The goal of these videos is to spread an archaic form of religion, but it is done through social media such as Twitter, YouTube, and Tumblr, which the Islamic State's influence agents are adept at using—they even create their own smartphone applications. The propaganda videos spread in this way are a horrifying mix of sadistic violence, the aesthetics of Hollywood action films, and video games. There are often compilations of scenes of murders in the style of online videogames that showcase shooting and selections of the "best killings."[88] This promotion is an effective means of filling their ranks with young men from every part of the world who come from various Islamic or religious cultural traditions and often live in difficult social conditions in immigrant communities. Jameson characterized video as a postmodern genre that is displacing the modernist genre of film. According to Heiser, the Islamic State's videos are evidence that the typical postmodern medium can be an instrument of effective propaganda for fundamentalist religion and premodern political visions and practices. According to this cultural theorist, the Islamic State creates a "perverse amalgam of technophilic pop-culture, meme-culture, and videogame styles along with archaic interpretations of religion, technicist-narcissistic-self-realization thinking and magical thinking, a professional image of propaganda, and archaic iconoclasm."[89] This hybrid isn't only something created by the Islamic State, but it also appears in various forms in other fundamentalist religious trends. Through social media, globalized culture in the styles of Hollywood films and videogames is becoming an instrument for a certain fundamentalist internationalism. Followers of the Islamic State or other radical Islamic religious communities come from different countries and cultures, but they share a common virtual world. A radical Islamist from Paris understands a fellow Islamist from Britain or Syria better than members of his local Islamic community, which is anchored in a certain specific tradition. Thanks to the global digital network, the Islamic State as an archaic form of Islam can become a universalist culture that separates itself from the traditional communities in individual countries. In a certain sense, the Islamic State is the exact opposite of the Identitarian movement, which rejects a universalist culture and wants to preserve and develop local cultural traditions. As Heiser emphasizes, part of the Islamic State's ideology is also an apocalyptic utopianism connected with a vision of renewing the "caliphate." The Islamic State evokes the idea of an impending world apocalypse and God's judgment and it behaves like a political and religious structure that has already begun to fulfill the vision of the "caliphate" as a government that is renewing the purity of Islam and saving it from the threatening apocalypse.[90] The Islamic State's utopianism mixes the premodern idea of a theocratic government with postmodern patterns and approaches, social media, Hollywood action films, and videogames.

The concept of hybridity or superhybridity that Heiser and other authors use in describing these cultural and political amalgams certainly has its justification, but it only expresses the phenomenal level of these formations. Hybridity is a term that describes the crossing of various elements (in biology, interspecies breeding). The authors who characterize these phenomena as hybrid touch upon the fact that postmodern political and cultural patterns are being crossed with premodern and modern patterns (e.g., the universalist nature of the Islamic State's virtual culture). However, these authors usually do not advance to the next interpretive level, at which they would show the show the internal relations between these patterns and their mutated character. This question is still awaiting further research into of the ideology of the Islamic State and similar fundamentalist religious movements.

Contemporary populism is a political formation that can be phenomenally described as hybrid. As I have demonstrated in more detail elsewhere, contemporary populism can be understood as a circulation between disparate political and cultural principles and practices.[91] On the one hand, there is a move toward further fragmentation of society into closed communities. This is a movement that Ihab Hassan views as an unintended consequence of the postmodernization of society. In my terminology, we're looking at a mutated form of the postmodernist pattern of radical plurality and paralogy. At the same time, there is a movement toward a certain unification on the basis of new forms of cultural, political, and social identity, as we were witnesses to in the emergence of the "people" and the "nation." This populism creates a political condition that both is and is not liberal-democratic, and at the same time both is and isn't authoritarian. Because of this intermediate state, I term the contemporary populism "metapopulism," where the prefix "meta-" expresses the term "methexis" as a designation of the space between two polarities (heaven and Earth, and the divine and the human in Plato's original use of the word). I derived this term from the neologism "metamodernism" that was introduced into cultural theory by Vermeulen and van den Akker. In these authors' view, there is an oscillation taking place in the present culture between postmodernism and modernism, as will be discussed in the following subchapter.

In metapopulism we also encounter other mutations of postmodernist concepts and approaches. Vladislav Surkov, for example, as one of the main creators of Vladimir Putin's political and ideological strategies, expresses himself in a manner that could be described as typically postmodern: he celebrates ceaseless change, processuality, the end of grand narratives, and the impossibility of truth. These patterns appear in his political strategies without their original emancipatory peripheral patterns, and they are connected with the current ideological, political, and economic interests of Russia. The postmodern rejection of the centrality of any kind of content ideology enables the Kremlin to switch discursive codes and address followers of disparate movements and political blocs. As a result, the Kremlin can reach right-wing nationalists who support Russia's opposition to the EU, radical leftists, who are attracted by the rejection of American hegemony, and religious conservatives who welcome the Kremlin's campaign against homosexuality.

A similar connection of postmodernist patterns with political interests appears in all kinds of various in many countries around the world. We can distinguish the different variations of metapopulism according to two basic perspectives. The first perspective is the character of the patterns to which the given variant is closer. Are they liberal-democratic patterns, or charismatic and authoritarian? Do postmodernist, modernist, or premodernist patterns dominate in it? For example, Macron's metapopulism is close to the patterns of liberal democracy and neoliberalism, but at the same time it contains elements referring to the symbols of the French Revolution as an expression of a republic identity along with a certain attempt at acting as the leader of republican France. The second perspective is the question of what is the political or general value horizon that determines the manner and direction of development of the postmodern patterns. For example, Sanders's and Corbyn's metapopulism developed the postmodernist principle of multiplicity of political and cultural identities and their horizon was the democratic-socialist. The radically conservative or neofascist horizon affects in the way in which postmodern patterns are politically developed by politicians such as Jörg Haider or the contemporary Identitarian movement that was discussed above. Thus, there are circulations between the postmodernist patterns and patterns influenced by given political interests and a certain political horizon. These circulations have no center, because metapopulism isn't tied to any ideology that would express a unified set of values, visions, and goals. Therefore, metapopulism can be imagined as a circulation between two poles or focal points.

A General Model of Contemporary Culture: Metamodernism

In the previous section we became acquainted with examples of phenomena that appear in various domains and display certain common traits. Cultural theorists mostly agree that these are formations composed of various elements that can be described as postmodernist, modernist, and premodernist. In describing them, they use terms such as hybridity, superhybridity, amalgam, assemblage, or mix, which record the phenomenal side of the formations but fail to capture the relationships among their elements and the process of how a given formation arises. Certain theorists do not limit themselves to this kind of phenomenal description and they deal with the genealogies and characteristics of these formations. The goal is to explain the origins of the formations that arrive after the end of postmodernism. Eshelman, Toth, Kirby and other theorists demonstrate on the basis of their genealogies how these formations are still postmodern and in what ways they no longer are postmodern. The first concept that progressed from a phenomenal description to an analysis of the structure of the relationships between the elements in a description of the overall situation was metamodernism, whose founding text with the title of "Notes on Metamodernism" was published in 2010. As mentioned before, its authors are the cultural theorists and art critics Robin van den Akker and Timotheus Vermeulen. Metamodernism represents a certain metatheory that relates previous theories of the end of postmodernism with the metamodernist model of contemporary culture. Since then, metamodernism has become a broader current in culture theory and art criticism, which produces texts on the manifestations of metamodernism in the fine arts, literature, sculpture, film, video, curating, and politics.[92] Metamodernist authors use the concept of the structure of experience, which enables them to track analogous changes in thinking and expression in fields that are distant from one another. Metamodernism represents a concept that captures essentially the entire area of culture and politics in their individual aspects, and at the same time it doesn't remain at the level of phenomenal description that's satisfied with the statement that a hybrid culture and politics is arising. Metamodernism has created a theoretical model that captures the general transformation of culture and politics that occurs independently in different places.

According to this conception, which was supported with abundant examples, we can describe the contemporary culture as methexis. In metamodernism there are fluctuations both toward the modernist patterns (in contemporary art this is illustrated, for example, through enthusiasm, a longing for the truth, earnestness, etc.), as well as fluctuations back to the postmodernist patterns (irony, relativism, play). Van den Akker and Vermeulen liken these oscillations to the movement of a pendulum that alternates between a first and second pole. Metamodernism thus, we repeat, absorbs both modernism and postmodernism, but it doesn't take either of them as its own starting point. According to van den Akker and Vermeulen, in the prevailing cultural and artistic current today the emerging modernist patterns (unity, the whole, purity, enthusiasm, empathy, hope, a longing for truth, etc.) cannot be reconciled with the postmodernist patterns (multiplicity, fragmentation, ambiguity, skepticism, apathy, melancholy, relativism, etc.) Their coexistence does not create, at least for now, the possibility of dialectical synthesis or harmonious conjunction. These authors, along with Bourriaud, perceive a networked character of the relations between individual poles (in Bourriaud's terminology, the relations between "island" in an "archipelago"), but unlike him, they do not believe that this network takes on the form of a living organism that harmonizes a nonviolent unification of individual "islands." Van den Akker and Vermeulen conceive of relations between the "islands" as a heterogeneous plurality that corresponds to Lyotard's concept of "negotiation" among heterogeneous discourses and to his conception of paralogy. Thus, the relationships between the modern and postmodern patterns exist, and we can understand them as network relationships, but these two types of patterns represent two heterogeneous codes and they continue to maintain their heterogeneity.[93] Postmodernist plurality and modernist unity or postmodernist fragmentation and the modernist conception of the whole create a variety of relationships and their contextual compositions in individual artistic or cultural formations, but this plurality or fragmentation doesn't change its heterogeneous status and the gap or chasm between them and the concept of unity or wholeness begins to close up.

It should be added that we can also find the antinomical relationship between the plurality and the unity that coexist within one formation in other domains, such as the domain of culture and art. In metapopulism an antinomical relationship appears between the unifying signifier (such as "Russian patriotism") and the multiplicity of demands and ideas in individual communities or opinion groups (such as the Orthodox Church, the movement to revive the "great Russian past," the Communist Party, left-wing movements, postmodern artists, etc.) I describe this antinomic relationship between unity and plurality as an allegorical type of signification, which is characterized by the fact that the general conception remains alienated from the individual phenomena that it "conceives," as is the case in Hegel's concept of allegory. Here there isn't the emergence of a universalism that is the result of hegemonization of a particular demand, as Ernesto Laclau describes in his works on populism. Instead, we are encountering a universalism without this hegemonization process and without a synthesizing relationship to the singular in its radical plurality. A similar relationship also appears in contemporary neoliberalism, in which the idea of the "whole economy" (the economy that requires self-sacrifice) remains separate from the interests and idea of the neoliberal subject, as we have seen in the chapter on the transformation of neoliberalism in the present stage of the interregnum.

In my view, the metamodernist conception of the relationship between unity and plurality, or generally between modernism and postmodernism, corresponds to the nature of the majority of the formations that are arising today in the domain of culture, art, politics, and economics. Exceptions are, for example, the tendency toward monism that Eshelman writes about (see above) and the "premodern" elements in radical orthodoxy. Vermeulen and van den Akker introduce a metamodernist model of the structure of experience, which creates the character of contemporary culture. It has two separate, heterogeneous poles, which are not possible to join in synthesis, and at the most general level of analysis they can be defined as modernism and postmodernism. In a more detailed description individual modernist and postmodernist patterns appear at the two poles. A constant oscillation arises between them, which does not stop at either of the two poles, and does not change the antinomical character of their relationship. The metamodernists describe this model using words, but we can illustrate it like this (Figure 2):

According to this model, we can observe in our culture that approaching one of the poles causes movement toward the opposite pole. As soon as an artist who is creating a work gets close to a unified organization of the individual elements in their work, they already start to be attracted to multiple and fragmentary processing of these elements. If the artist's work begins to be too similar to postmodern fragmented compositions, they feel a longing to unify them and create a whole. The metamodernists thus assume that multiplicity or unity, as well as other postmodernist and modernist patterns, exhibit a certain repulsive force that prevents an artist from identifying with either one or the other pattern and makes them a central axis of their creation. None of these patterns becomes a goal that an artist will pursue persistently—their fulfillment is always only temporary. Vermeulen and van den Akker, as well as other cultural theorists, speak of the neo-romanticism of contemporary culture, by which

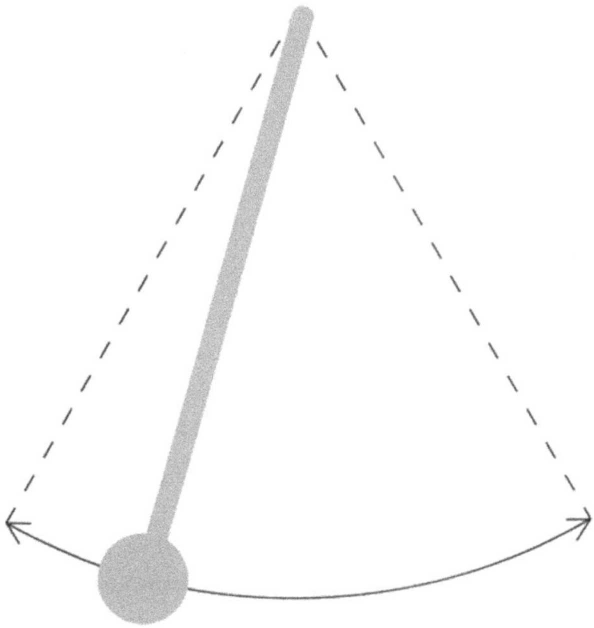

Figure 2 Model of the metamodernist conception of contemporary culture © Michael Hauser.

they mean that the desire for a certain idea or pattern is never fulfilled. The unfulfillability is caused by the fact that the given idea or pattern has a greater repulsive force the closer we get to it. We can conceive of this repulsive force in various ways; for example, as an expression of social and cultural hysteria, which Žižek connects with a Lacanian desire that can never identify with its object-cause. According to Žižek, the hysterical character of contemporary culture is manifested, for instance, in cyberspace through confusion, uncertainty, and constant questioning of what cyberspace expects of us.[94] Vermeulen and van den Akker describe the state of culture which is characterized by a phenomenon that I term disidentification; that is, disconnection from a certain object or idea which, however, we can already find in postmodern culture.[95] The difference compared with postmodern culture consists in postmodern culture identifying in a certain way with multiplicity, fragmentation, decentralization, and other postmodernist patterns. It is an identification that's weakened by the presence of peripheral patterns. In contemporary culture, two parallel processes are taking place: a disidentification with postmodernist patterns along with a desire for identification with modernist patterns (the metamodernists are not thinking about a role for premodern patterns). A strange paradox of the postmodern subject appears here. A disidentification of ideas with a certain general principle is an expression of postmodern skepticism and cynicism, which is one of the basic postmodern patterns. The postmodern subject identifies with these patterns (in a weakened form), and therefore also identifies with disidentification. In contemporary culture, a disidentification with postmodernist patterns is taking place, and therefore we can speak about a disidentification taking place with regard to the pattern of disidentification itself. However, in contemporary culture, this process usually does not lead to identification with modernist patterns. A Hegelian dialectic is not developing, nor is an antinomical dialectic, in which the dialectical movement remains fixed in a certain intermediate position. Identification does not arise as a negation of disidentification. Negation does not provoke a process (identification) that would arrive at its realization and completion; that is, at a state when we truly identify with a particular modernist idea.

In my book *Paths from Postmodernism* [*Cesty z postmodernismu*] and in the essay "Beyond the Boundaries of Postmodernism" [Za hranice postmodernismu], I have described this intermediate state with the help of Marcel Blanchot's concept of "neutral space," which expresses a space that does not belong either to being or to non-being, and a dialectics of opposites does not operate within it. The subject is in a certain asubjective state, where it finds itself in the movements between various poles, which it always looks upon from a certain detached position.[96] According to my conception of the origin of the subject after the end of postmodernism that I introduced in these texts, its movement to the limit can take place on the basis of an act of radical negation with the neutral space not disappearing, because it creates a basis against which the subject is continually defined and thus it maintains its identification with ideas. In my opinion, Ihab Hassan came up with a similar idea when he writes about the "via negative" that consists in the completion of the negation of the given forms of knowledge and values brought by modernism, but it isn't consistent enough in this negation. With this radicalized postmodern negation, the subject enters a state of "kenosis," which is the complete liberation from its bonds to particular values. In my terminology, therefore, it has achieved a complete disidentification. According to Hassan, the state of radical negation and kenosis is a condition for creating a relationship to reality and to ideas such as the idea of truth, the idea of planetary citizenship, and so on. Radical negation and kenosis create the ability to identify with values and ideas, such as trust.[97]

In this way, Hassan creates his conception of fiduciary realism, which was discussed in another context above. The metamodernist authors correctly describe the oscillation that is taking place in contemporary culture between poles that indicate that a complete process of identification is not taking place because this process is blocked in some way. This state corresponds to Blanchot's neutral space or the state of kenosis that Hassan writes about.

The Shortcomings of the Metamodernist Model

I consider Vermeulen and van den Akker's metamodernist model of contemporary culture, which captures the oscillations between antinomical poles as the first model to capture the cultural tendencies expressed in various ways within individual conceptions of culture after the end of modernism. However, this model has certain shortcomings.

Its first shortcoming is that it only describes the structure of experience, but it leaves the production of individual formations after the end of postmodernism unexamined. As have already seen, although we find postmodernist and modernist patterns in individual cultural and political formations, some of these formations are closer to postmodernist patterns, while others are closer to the modernist ones. Therefore, these formations do not arise in the way the metamodernist model believes. We determine upon a closer analysis that the oscillations do not occur at the same distances from each pole. The second shortcoming of metamodernism is it disregards the premodern elements that are demonstrably present in certain intellectual, cultural, and political phenomena, such as the Identitarian movement and radical orthodoxy. And finally, metamodernism's third shortcoming is that it does not explain the genesis and character of metamodernism itself in relation to postmodernism. This model gives the impression that contemporary culture is specific in that we find an oscillation between modernism and postmodernism in it. However, haven't similar oscillations already taken place in postmodernist culture? At least, according to some theorists, such as Toth, modernism also operated within postmodernism. Also, according to my epicyclic model of postmodernism, oscillations or circulations were taking place between both poles, although it was happening in a different way than we see in contemporary culture.

The Elliptical Model of Contemporary Culture

The shortcomings of metamodernism call for us to elaborate a different model of contemporary culture. I propose a model that stems from metamodernism but attempts to deal with its shortcomings. This is a model that utilizes the properties of the ellipse. The ellipse differs from the epicycloid in that it has two focal points, neither of which is dominant, and this allows us to illustrate the fundamental characteristic of contemporary culture, which was described by metamodernism. This characteristic is the coexistence of two poles, of postmodernism and modernism (or in certain cases, premodernism). There is neither a relationship nor a hierarchy between these poles, because neither of them creates a dominant code. It is this feature of contemporary culture that is appropriately illustrated in the two focal points inside the ellipse. The shape of the ellipse is defined as a multiplicity of the points that have a constant sum of distances from both focal points. Each point on the perimeter has a different distance from the two focal points, but it also has one common trait with all the other points: the sum of distances from both of the focal points. This property of the ellipse aptly illustrates that the formations arising in contemporary culture have differing distances from postmodernism and modernism (or premodernism). In other words, certain postmodernist patterns are stronger or weaker in particular formations, and the same is true for modernist or premodernist patterns. A common trait of all these formations we have encountered is the fact that they have a relationship to both of the poles described here. Another quality of the ellipse is that it can be understood in relation to a circle or an epicycloid. The epicycloid as an illustration of the character of culture in the first period of the interregnum changes into a circle if the peripheral movements around the inner perimeter of the circle disappear. This occurs because the peripheral patterns relating to the evental traces in the domain of art and politics have ceased operating. The circle then turns into an ellipse if a bifurcation of its central point takes place and it becomes two focal points. The ellipse displays an "eccentric" anomaly of the circle, and for this reason I propose that the ellipse offers us a more appropriate illustration of contemporary culture than metamodernism's oscillating model (Figure 3).

In this illustration of the ellipse, the symbols *P* and *M* represent the focal points that represent postmodernism and modernism, where the focal point *M* can also represent premodernism. The symbols F_1 and F_2 express individual cultural or political formations at various distances from postmodernism and

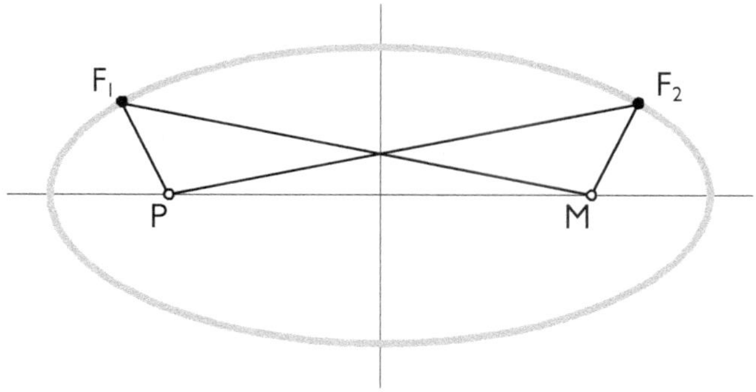

Figure 3 The ellipse as a model of contemporary culture (in the second period of the interregnum) © Michael Hauser.

modernism or premodernism. The appropriate term for movement around these focal points is circulation, and not metamodernist oscillation, which is connected with the idea of a pendulum that swings from one side to the other.

For example, Stuckism can be interpreted as a set of concepts and approaches that arise in circulations between two focal points that comprise, for instance, the modernist pattern of the artistic trend as an "-ism" and the postmodernist pattern of a decentralized network. This is how Stuckism can come to characterize itself as an "international non-movement." This concept can then be placed into point F_1 on the outer circumference of the ellipse. We can define it as having a shorter distance from the postmodernist pattern (*P*) than its distance from the modernist pattern (*M*). However, its character is formed by the relationship to both patterns that make up the focal points in the ellipse. This concept is not the result of identification with one of these patterns, and therefore is missing a center or a pattern that would enable an adequate interpretation of it, so the Stuckist movement is not merely a decentralized network. It is closer to the pattern of multiplicity in the form of a decentralized network and farther away from the pattern of a modernist unity as a particular movement with a clear definition of its boundaries (i.e., a modernist "-ism"). It is not merely a decentralized network because Stuckism relates to certain manifestos, which makes it reminiscent of a modernist artistic movement. It is a decentralized network with manifestos. For comparison: we can place radical realism at point F_2, because its distance from the postmodern pattern (*P*) is greater than its distance from the modernist pattern (*M*), as evidenced in the analysis above.

It is possible in this way to describe, in principle, all the formations that I have discussed in more detail: digimodernism, altermodernism, the Identitarian movement, radical realism, radical orthodoxy, metamodernism, and so on. The eccentricity of the ellipse can be understood as an illustration of the fact that more or less all of these formations have a description inadequate to their character, as was discussed at the beginning of this section. The circulations around the circumference of the ellipse create formations that cannot be adequately described through patterns that occupy the position of focal points. It is the basic nature of symbolic production in the present stage of the interregnum. As I wrote above, this concerns the connection of two semantic structures: neither-nor, and both-and. The ellipse creates a model that captures both of these structures, and this is why I name the present cultural production "elliptical" in relation to these structures. This form of symbolic production characterizes the present situation in culture and cultural theory.

The Contemporary Situation and Three Forms of Elliptical Circulation: Reactive, Obscure, and Pre-evental

Theorists of contemporary culture draw attention to the problem of whether emerging patterns and approaches are a renewal of modernist patterns or instead they are patterns that are reminiscent of modernism but not identical to its patterns. For example, Lee Konstantinou generally argues that in today's literature there is a desire arising for a renewal of what postmodernism disrupted or deconstructed.[98] On the other hand, Josh Toth and Neil Brooks write that "pre-postmodern" patterns are emerging that are not a direct return, but in many regards are formed from postmodernism itself. Hence, the mourning for a political horizon such as radical difference that we see in the late Derrida, who does not express a desire for a simple return of what already was.[99] Euphoria, empathy, earnestness, postirony, authenticity, depth, a longing for unity and truth, and other traits and tendencies that appear in contemporary culture are combined by certain theorists and trends with a call for a new universalism or an emancipatory project (Bourriaud, Hassan), but in others, by contrast, there is a radical critique of universalism and instead radically conservative ideas about creating a culturally purified European identity are expressed (de Benoist and the Identitarian movement).

Postmodernist patterns and their mutations do not generally appear in theories of the end of postmodernism, and we have examined several of these theories above. The mutations are created through a connection of postmodernist patterns of various kinds that come from various domains in society. An example of an economic-social mutation is contemporary neoliberalism, in which the mutation of the postmodernist concept of singularity has mutated into the absolute responsibility of the singularity. Another example was the mutation of the postmodern pattern of multiplicity and plurality into a self-centered identity, tribalism, and fundamentalism, as Hassan has written.[100] It was caused by a whole complex of factors starting with the feeling of a loss of identity, anxiety, and ending with economic and social pressure to dissolve social cohesion under the influence of hyperindividualism, which has been discussed from a different perspective by Lipovetsky.[101] We meet with the technological mutation of postmodernist patterns in social media and the digital world, as Kirby writes. An example of political mutation was the Identitarian movement with its concepts of ethnodifferentialism and metapopulism which used the concepts of multiplicity, paralogy, and so on, as conceptual models of political strategies. Another example of the political mutation of postmodernism was the Islamic State, which Jörg Heiser describes as an amalgam of pop-culture, videogames, and an archaic conception of religion.

As has already been said, postmodernist patterns have a prosthetic and promiscuous character. After the extinction of the original emancipatory and modernist peripheral patterns the direction of their transformation depends on patterns and horizons that postmodernism connects with. There is a production of formations here that has the character of an elliptical circulation between two focal points. One focal point represents postmodern patterns, and the other represents patterns that belong to various economic, technological, political, or cultural trends. These formations can only be distinguished according to whether they are economic, technological, and so on, but also according to what kind of direction they are taking. Badiou's terminology can help us make this distinction. In certain formations, we find a phenomenon that Badiou terms "reactive novelty," and it corresponds to a formation called the "reactive subject." Other formations have a nature reminiscent of the "obscure subject." In Badiou's view, the reactive subject is defined by the fact that it creates new phenomena that are supposed to cover or negate the evental traces in the given present time. As an example, he cites the French Group of New Philosophers (André Glucksmann), who created the intellectual apparatus for legitimizing the unfettered capital and global domination of the United States.[102] The obscure subject manifests itself in also creating a certain new phenomenon that is an ahistorical and anti-event body, which is supposed to represent a full and transparent embodiment of a certain idea or conception, such as fundamentalist ideas of God, race, or the nationalists' understanding of the nation. Badiou cites Islamic fundamentalism as an example of an obscure subject, which covers or obscures the presence of emancipatory elements in society. It obscures these emancipatory elements by replacing them with its own anti-evental conception or idea which acts or gives the effect of a transcendence.[103]

On the basis of these concepts from Badiou we can create the terms "reactive formation" and "obscure formation" of the interregnum. An example of a reactive formation could be de Benoist's conception of ethnopluralism or the Identitarian movement, which negates the emancipatory elements from 1968, as we can see in the overall rejection of the generation connected with the 1968 movement. The Islamic State can serve as example of an obscure formation that replaced the emancipatory elements that were activated in the Arab countries in the form of "Arab socialism" with archaic ideas about God and religion. Although ethnopluralism contains ideas of a culturally organic society, as I wrote above, this is an idea connected with the movement of difference between individual cultures and thus it lacks the kind of full and transparent form seen in fundamentalist ideas about God. This is why I classify ethnopluralism and the Identitarian movement among the reactive formations, even though we find ideas of an organic society there. This is how we can distinguish between reactive political formations and obscure religious-political ones. They are the result of two types of production in the present period of the interregnum, in which we encounter mutated postmodernist patterns. These two types of production arise as circulations between postmodernist patterns and patterns that are either reactive or obscure in their orientation.

However, there is also a third type of elliptical circulation that produces formations of a different kind. This circulation takes place between postmodernist patterns and patterns that can be related to event element in the past or present. Certain hypotheses or anticipations of their future forms appear in them. In the domain of politics it's the emancipatory elements that Badiou connects with the idea or hypothesis of communism as an egalitarian social principle. These elements are beginning to appear in a variety of forms in contemporary culture and theory. As van den Akker and Vermeulen show, the figure of "utopia" is again emerging in today's art, whether as an individual longing or a collective idea. This "utopian impulse" (Jameson) lacks a clearly defined form and usually doesn't represent a clearly articulated political stance. The emergence of the figure of utopia expresses the generally shared feeling of the young generation that today's world is full of inequalities and exploitation.[104] It's a sense of life that finds various political expressions and embodiments, for example, the new social movements that have arisen since about the beginning of the new millennium which band together under the motto "another world is possible." Ihab Hassan writes about the need to deepen postmodernism by connecting it with a sense for a certain universal emancipatory dimension that he conceives of as planetary citizenship.[105] In political philosophy we are witnessing a return to the conception of communism as a certain necessary hypothesis that enables us to reflect on the limits of global capitalism and to maintain the idea of a society that overcomes the fundamental inequalities, exploitation, and privatization of freedom.[106] Today, it is no longer bound to its previous incarnation. Authors such as Alain Badiou, Slavoj Žižek, Michael Hardt, Antonio Negri, Jean-Luc Nancy, Jacques Rancière, and Gianni Vattimo, although they come from different philosophical postulates, understand it as a certain hypothesis that so far has lacked definitive outlines. This open conception of communism is part of the interregnum, even though it is beyond its boundaries because its hypothetical future incarnation would mean that we find ourselves outside the interregnum. The idea of communism expresses emancipatory elements scattered in various configurations in contemporary culture as well as in past cultures. As we have seen above, their significance was extinguished in the 1970s and 1980s and the sequence in which its concrete historical incarnations were operating closed. In this open conception of communism, which is part of the interregnum situation, we find a multiplicity of elements that have their beginnings not only in the modern period but also in the premodern one. For example, Hardt and Negri's understanding of communism as a society founded on a commons draws from premodern forms of ownership, such as *obschchina* ownership. Therefore, in the analysis of this pro-evental cultural production we cannot satisfy ourselves with a model based upon the concept of postmodernism and modernism, because certain elements here are premodern. An elliptical circulation arises here whose defining trait is not the absence of premodern patterns, but the presence of elements that are emancipatory and it's possible to relate them to the plurality of scattered communist elements found in modernism and premodernism. This elliptical circulation produces cultural and political formations that contain pre-evental elements or horizons, and these elements enter into relation with other patterns such as postmodernist patterns (multiplicity, difference, etc.), modernist patterns (a secular concept of unity, organization, concentration, etc.) or even premodern patterns (e.g., the premodern conception of artistic realism or *obschchina* ownership). Circulation associated with the relevant type of cultural production prepares, at least hypothetically, the conditions for the emergence of a new event in art and politics which ends the period of the interregnum, and therefore I term it pre-evental.

We can also classify radical realism in this category, because it shows a circulation between postmodernist, modernist, and classical premodern patterns. It differs from reactive or obscure premodernism because it develops motifs that contain radical humanist elements connected with the depiction of human beings and their world in classical art, as Lukács and Lifšic write. Radical realist painters discover an anticipation of unalienated social relations in classical art, which should become an element of the new incarnation of the communist idea.

Enthusiasm, affect, a sense for unity, community, truth, and other phenomena are appearing in today's politics. These patterns can appear in all three types of elliptical circulation. For example, we find enthusiasm and affect in reactive circulations, such as in the Identitarian movement, and we also find them in the obscure circulation of the Islamic State's fighters and the pre-evental circulation, such as in American democratic socialists. We can thus speak of reactive affect, obscure affect, and pre-evental affect—and the same is true for the other patterns as well. Each of these patterns that theorists of the end of postmodernism have written about are necessary to interpret with a regard to which type of circulation they appear in.

However, there is a number of phenomena where it is difficult to determine which type of circulation they belong to. This ambiguity is due to the fact that we are not in a situation where we could establish the lines of generic procedures and where we have their authoritative names available. We are in an interregnum in which there are only scattered traces of past truths, if we have managed to prevent their extinction, and besides these remnants there are only hypotheses of the possibility of future truth-events. These scattered traces with unclear names are not a sufficient guide that would enable us to distinguish between individual types of circulation. For example, where do we classify Stuckist realism in painting? Stuckism is an example of a return of modern realism that wants to renew the spiritual conception of the reality of certain early modernists. Is it a reactive type of circulation, or an obscure one? Or can we conceive of Stuckism as a pre-evental circulation?

Despite these ambiguities, which will always be present in a period of interregnum, it is still worthwhile to distinguish among these three types of circulations because this is how we can create orientation points to use in determining the position and direction of movement of individual formations. We can characterize the current situation as the second stage of the interregnum, in which we are too far from the evental traces that were operating through the peripheral patterns in the domains of economics, culture, and politics in the first stage of the interregnum. The current stage of the interregnum is a period in which reactive or obscure directions for the movement of culture and society appear as more likely than evental movement. It isn't possible to decide whether the hypothesis of the advent of a truth-event in the future will not remain only a hypothesis. The present interregnum is a period which—due to its distance from past truth-events—gives rise to the idea that there will only ever be circulation movements that run forever that never turn into the fulfillment of the promises they evoke.

Part Two of the book is dedicated to Badiou's philosophy, which disrupts these generally shared ideas and changes the coordinates in which we reflect on the present situation: Badiou's philosophy creates the conditions for an exodus from the interregnum.

Part Two

Badiou's Transitive Ontology

Introduction

The Philosophy of Truths as a Response to the Interregnum

In Part One, I described the current situation in the domains of culture, politics, and economics as a second period of the interregnum, in which the effects of previous truth-events are no longer operating, but where at the same time, formations are arising in which various patterns emerge that are reminiscent of modernism or premodernism. According to theorists of contemporary culture, these are patterns that arise as reactions to neoliberal globalization, to the institutionalization of postmodernism, and to the general uncertainty and anxiety in contemporary society. These "new" patterns are not tied to an event and its generic effects but are part of a reactive, obscure, or pre-evental circulation. As stated above, I base my conception of the interregnum on Badiou's conception of the interval that exists between two sequences of the fundamentally egalitarian idea called communism, which gives rise to effects in the political, cultural, and economic domains. I consider this conception to be a new manner of orientation in the given situation, which can be understood in a certain sense as a new version of the cognitive mapping that Jameson recommended at the end of the 1980s to those who were seeking a way to find themselves and formulate their position in a system within the world of postmodern randomness. In the previous part of the book, we encountered a wide range of cultural, political, and economic phenomena that display certain similarities, even though they do not directly influence one another. We also find these traits in Badiou's philosophy; however, in comparison with other contemporary theories, Badiou's philosophy is characterized by the fact that it was formed as a set of answers to the conscious situation of the interregnum or "interval." Badiou's monumental work can then be interpreted as a philosophy that has been raising the question since the 1980s of how to understand the age that arrived after the closure of the twentieth century's sequence and what position to take in it. The theorists of contemporary culture that I discussed in the previous part of the book came up with their conceptions around the year 2000; that is, in the period before the end of postmodernism. However, their efforts to name the current situation mostly remained at the level of sub-concepts, such as fiduciary realism, monism, or the archipelago model. They are reacting to the end of postmodernism, but Badiou focuses on the end of the sequence of truth-events, which he claims took place at the end of the 1970s. In the 1970s and 1980s, the future dominant elements of the first stage of the interregnum (postmodernism, neoliberalism, and liberal democracy) arise in the space of the extinguishing evental traces. Badiou implicitly conceives of postmodernism as a form of interval or interregnum. He doesn't state this explicitly, but from his understanding of postmodern philosophy as lacking truths, we can conclude that he considers the emergence of postmodern philosophy to be one of the responses to the end of the sequence of the idea of communism. This answer is that Lyotard and other postmodern philosophers interpreted the end of this sequence as the end of "grand narratives" which made universalist demands accompanied by violence against the singular. We will return to Badiou's assessment of postmodern philosophy later, but now it's clear how he differs from postmodern philosophy. Badiou situates his philosophy in the same period as postmodern philosophy, but in contrast with it, he understands this period as an interval between two sequences of the communist idea with its future sequence merely forming a "communist hypothesis" in the same sense as Pascal's wager. Postmodern philosophers generally perceive this period as the beginning of an era when postmodern culture is spreading and society frees itself of the violence of metaphysics and ideologies, although Derrida's warning voice predicted that after the closing of the radically emancipatory horizon, the destructive tendencies of capitalist globalism would intensify. According to Lyotard and other postmodern philosophers, this period brings relief from the metaphysical violence coming from the past, which they also connect with the concept of truth.

In Part One of the book, I demonstrated that postmodern theory and culture are connected with the extinguishing traces of the communist idea and with peripheral modernist patterns. This is the circumstance that Badiou doesn't take into account in his assessment of postmodernism because he's mainly focusing on the postmodern annulment of the significance of truth. My basic thesis was that postmodernism is not a new epoch, but rather the first stage of an interregnum. As soon as the communist and modernist elements become extinct and cease operating, the postmodern patterns become dependent on other patterns and horizons that cause their mutations and determine the direction of their development. This can be so contradictory that it is hardly even possible to speak about how postmodernism has founded a new epoch. However, we can only recognize this promiscuous character of postmodernism in the present stage of the interregnum, when we encounter various forms of mutated postmodernism after postmodernism joined up with neoliberalism, institutions, the Identitarian movement, the Islamic State—and we could make the list even longer. In the 1980s, however, this nature of postmodernism wasn't yet evident and it wasn't possible to argue in this vein. When Badiou speaks of his wager on the hypothesis of communism, and generally about the wager on truth, he is expressing the situation in the 1980s when, based on historical and cultural analyses, it was impossible in principle to decide whether we were entering a new era or an interregnum was about to begin. Badiou's periodization, which is the opposite of the periodization that we deduce from Lyotard or other postmodern philosophers, develops out of this wager on the communist hypothesis and on truth. What is the beginning of the historical interval or the interregnum for Badiou is for Lyotard a moment of relief at the end of the grand narratives and the beginning of a postmodern society that is breaking away from a unifying universalism. Badiou contends that Lyotard's critique of the revolutionary "grand narratives" of the last two centuries enables the restoration of monstrous inequalities and an ideology of finiteness. The postmodern criticism of all "greatness" deprives us of a "positive imaginary" that necessarily accompanies the process of emancipation.[1]

Contemporary cultural theorists mostly rely on the periodization that classifies postmodernism as an independent epoch that is now ending. It turns out that only now we're entering a certain intervening period in which new cultural patterns have not yet been stabilized. From the perspective of Badiou's periodization, the end of postmodernism is merely an ending of a particular period that arose at the end of the previous emancipatory sequence. However, this end is not the beginning of a new cultural epoch; instead, it's the beginning of a new stage in the development of the interregnum, in which pre-evental or pre-communist circulations arise, as well as reactive or obscure circulations. However, Badiou had already developed a theory at the end of the 1980s which itself represented a certain end of postmodernism: *Badiou avant la lettre*. The book *Being and Event* was published in the original French in 1988 and in English translation in 2005. At the beginning of the millennium, Badiou's theory was discovered in universities outside of France, and it began to attract the attention of critical circles at these universities who were growing dissatisfied with the work of Derrida and other poststructuralist authors whose theories had become academic canons detached from new social and political phenomena. One of the manifestations of the change in the intellectual atmosphere in the university environment, which Simon Critchley described as a symptom of the end of postmodernism, was that students began studying Badiou and Rancière as a certain expression of disagreement with the postmodern academic establishment. The theorists of the end of postmodernism that I've written about in Part One of the book have been changing the intellectual and cultural terrain since the beginning of the millennium, and they are creating more or less elaborated thought sketches that will be answers to the end of postmodernism.

However, Badiou had already declared the end of postmodernism in the 1980s in his philosophy. He did this by starting to develop conceptions that in many ways transcended the boundaries of postmodernism. For example, his conceptions of truth, events, universalism, the subject, and fidelity are topics that cultural theorists today treat as signs of the end of postmodernism. In *Being and Event*, Badiou already considered postmodernism as obsolete in its practice of depleting the conception of truth. In this book, he heralds the beginning of a new period of ontological "doctrines of truth," which differ from previous conceptions of truth in that truth is separated from knowing. Badiou differs from most contemporary theorists of the end of postmodernism because he doesn't infer the beginning of the new period from cultural and social phenomena like the change in the "structure of experience" in art, the advent of clusters of crises and apocalyptic events, or a sociologically discernible change in attitudes and values. Badiou's proclamation of the end of postmodernism in the question of truth is not based on empirical circumstances, sociological studies, or analyses of tendencies in contemporary art, but instead from breakthrough discoveries in mathematics, especially in set theory. What he particularly has in mind is Paul Cohen's groundbreaking discovery of the generic set and the method of forcing in the 1960s. In these discoveries, Badiou recognized the possibility of a new understanding of ontology ("mathematics is ontology"), and he created a conception of truth as a generic procedure connected with events.[2] The end of postmodernism, at least in the question of truth, arrives when philosophy discovers or has the will to discover breakthroughs in the development of science (mathematics) which change the external conditions of philosophy and enable the philosophical claim that "truths exist." The end of postmodernism then consists in the fact that it loses its monopoly on producing theses on truth and philosophical works appear that establish a certain new boundary. This is the boundary between a postmodern sophistic philosophy or culture in which truths do not exist and a philosophy or culture that wagers on the existence of truths. This boundary creates an intellectual space that is at the same time also a space of negotiation, which lies outside postmodernism. Badiou writes that truth is becoming a new word in Europe and beyond.[3]

These words can be understood as a certain anticipation of a renewed relationship to the concept of truth that Ihab Hassan and other theorists of the end of postmodernism spoke about nearly two decades later. In this sense, Badiou is the first theorist of the end of postmodernism because he creates a theory that in itself evokes the end of postmodernism as a culturally dominating element that gives the impression that the concept of truth has become universally impossible. Of course, this does not mean that postmodernism ceases to operate as a set of patterns that express and give shape to philosophical thinking, art, and the character of cultural production, but it is a disqualification of the unstated postmodern demand for its own universal validity that we can express at the most general level as the thesis "every truth is relative" (socially or culturally constructed, textual, deconstructable, etc.). This is not just a simple liar's paradox such as "Epimenides says that all Cretans are liars. Epimenides is a Cretan" or "this sentence isn't true," which would indict postmodernism as a logical paradox (the sentence "every truth is relative" is relative, and therefore admits its own negation; therefore, not every truth is truly relative). Such a logical critique of postmodernism misses the logic of cultural phenomena, which do not arise as the result of logical reasoning, but are ways of thinking, manifesting, and negotiating that arise in complex interactions between political events, economic conditions, and clusters of crises or the emptying of the previous culture. For Badiou, the end of postmodernism means *creating* the possibility of not thinking, not manifesting, and not behaving in ways dependent on postmodern thought structures. The end of postmodernism consists in breaking through the wall of universalized relativism that at one time didn't appear to be a wall but the breaking demolition of all walls. This hole smashed into the wall of postmodernism can but doesn't have to be used in the foreseeable future as a passageway into the unknown space behind the wall, but at the very least, it acts as an element of awareness that the opening exists. Another effect can also occur. This breakthrough creates the awareness that there is a wall around us. Postmodernism first appears like the demolition of all walls and gives the impression that its basic trait is to continue breaking every wall down into ruins. It is only when someone makes a breakthrough within postmodernism itself that we notice that it has also become a wall. It is this awareness that postmodernism acts as a wall that causes the end of postmodernism as a culturally dominant form that, so to speak, internalizes itself in human beings.

1

Situating Badiou in the Interregnum

Do Truths Exist in the Interregnum? The Mysteries of Badiou's Philosophy

In the introductory chapter of the book, I dealt with the prehistory of the interregnum, in which the traces of truth procedures are becoming extinct. However, Badiou has created work that shows how we are at the beginning of a new "doctrine of truth." It seems that there is a contradiction between two hypotheses of how to situate Badiou in the interregnum, and we can formulate them as two theses.

THESIS A: Badiou's philosophy belongs among the formations of the interregnum which show circulations between unity and plurality, between truth and the impossibility of its full presence, and so on.

THESIS B: Badiou's philosophy has created a new beginning of a "doctrine of truths," but it doesn't show a circulation typical for formations in the interregnum. Badiou's philosophy represents a formation that, because of its structure, does not arise from the interregnum and only belongs to it because it arose in the conditions of the interregnum.[1]

This contradiction is related to how Badiou understands philosophy and the conditions of its existence. According to Badiou, philosophy depends on external conditions; that is, on the existence of truths in all four domains where truths can appear (science, politics, art, and love). Badiou clearly formulates this position in *Manifesto for Philosophy*, where we read that philosophy doesn't exist in all historical arrangements, but only appears under specific conditions, and these conditions are the existence of truths as generic procedures.[2] Badiou admits that there are societies without one or more truths: societies that lack mathematics, or others where art is so interconnected with holy functions that it's inaccessible to us, and then there are societies where love is absent or inexpressible, and societies where despotism is the natural state and politics do not appear.[3]

According to Badiou, philosophy arises only when all four types of truth, or four types of its conditioning, exist together. Philosophy does not create the truths that condition it, as Badiou argues in *Being and Event*. Philosophy occupies a position that in itself must remain at a certain unique distance from truth procedures. This is because it acts as a meta-ontology in relation to mathematics as an ontology, as a meta-politics in relation to political truths, as a meta-art in relation to artistic truths, and as a meta-relationship theory in relation to events. Badiou asks whether at least one philosophical statement can meaningfully be declared to be true.[4] Badiou calls this close connection philosophy's suturing to its conditions. For instance, in the nineteenth century—in the period between Hegel and Nietzsche—philosophy got closer to science and thus took on a positivist and scientistic form. In the same period, philosophy in the form of Marxism moved into its political condition: revolutionary change was to be the realization of philosophy and also its end.[5]

The decisive question is whether in today's world we can find truth procedures; that is, external conditions that enable the "gesture of recomposition of philosophy."[6] If these conditions are not present, Thesis A (above) should be valid. Badiou's philosophy would thus show a circulation typical for interregnum formations. However, if these truths do not exist, could Thesis B be true? Badiou's philosophy would exist as an exception because, in his words, philosophy depends on its conditions of truth in science, politics, art, and love. If we cannot find these truths in the interregnum, the position of Badiou's philosophy is then a mystery. How did this position appear if there aren't truths as conditions for it to arise? Or do truths still operate in the interregnum?

Badiou answers this crucial question ambiguously. In *Manifesto for Philosophy*, he claims that a renewal of philosophy forces a "uniqueness of events" that are tied to the four truth procedures: in science, set theory (Cantor, Gödel, Cohen); in politics, it's the political ingenuity of the unambiguous events between 1965 and 1980 (the Chinese Cultural Revolution, May 1968 in France, the Polish Solidarity movement, etc.); in art, Badiou names the poets Pessoa, Mandelstam, and Celan; and he singles out Lacan's discoveries in the concept of love.[7] It appears that in Badiou's conception we find ourselves at the beginning of a new period in which all four types of external conditions for the renewal of philosophy exist, and that we are in a situation which is actually not an interval or interregnum because all four types of truth procedures are operating. A state of interregnum would be a period in which we simply are unaware that the truths continue to exist. And if we acknowledged the presence of truths and continued to develop their generic procedures, the interregnum would end. In this case, the interregnum would be a state of denial and displacement of truths that had not ceased operating.

However, Badiou does not see the interregnum as a state where truths are pushed out of our consciousness. As we have seen in the introductory section dedicated to the prehistory of the interregnum, Badiou writes that we find ourselves in an interval after the end of one historical sequence of the communist idea, whose last incarnation is the political events of the 1960s and 1970s that were discussed there. We are in the interval or the interregnum in which these political truth procedures have been extinguished, their sequence has closed, and thus the external conditions for the renewal of philosophy have passed. Badiou thus introduces a certain divide between the present situation, termed an interval, the sequence—this supports Thesis A, that Badiou's philosophy is an interregnum formation and we find the previously described circulation as its typical trait. However, at the same time, Badiou refers to the truths of all four types and he understands his philosophy as a renewal of the "doctrine of truths." Badiou thus situates his philosophy in such a way that it corresponds to the first part of Thesis B, according to which it is not an interregnum formation, but neither does it correspond to the thesis that we are in an interval situation where the sequence of truths has closed. It would follow from this that Badiou's philosophy is conditioned by truth procedures that have closed. There would be a conditioning relationship between his philosophy and these truths, but at the same time, there is also a caesura present in this relationship. Although the truths condition the philosophy and enable a gesture of its renewal, at the same time these are truths that have closed. This paradoxical relationship of philosophy to truths is among the greatest mysteries of Badiou's philosophy, which has thus far eluded the attention of his interpreters.[8] It is related to another mystery that will appear later, which is the existence of the subject in the interregnum. The subject is defined by operations of fidelity to the truth-event. If these truth-events have closed, can a subject arise in the interregnum? And if it can, what is this subject faithful to? In the last chapter of the book, I argue that these mysteries were one of the motives for Badiou creating the conceptions contained in his book *The Immanence of Truths*, in which I believe he has managed to solve these mysteries. These mysteries faded before most of Badiou's interpreters registered them and before they paid due attention to them.

Now it becomes necessary to more closely investigate the divide between the interregnum and individual truth procedures. In other words, we will deal with the closing of truth procedures from the perspective of Badiou's philosophy.

First, we'll focus on the closing of the political truth procedure, which creates a divide that defines the interval period or interregnum. Then we'll investigate this divide in artistic truth and the truth of love. Scientific truth, specifically, the truth procedure of set theory, will be the subject of a further subchapter where its special character will be revealed.

The Closing of Political Truths

We can already see the closing of political truth procedures in Badiou's book *Theory of the Subject*, which he started writing in the 1970s and early 1980s. In it, Badiou deals with the historical periodization of emancipatory politics in relation to Marxism. He views Marxism as a militant politics that had a new stage opened for it with the Russian Revolution of 1917. Although Leninist politics won out, it never managed to find an answer to the problem that is inscribed in the conflict between the state and the revolution. Leninist parties joined forces with the institution of the state in order to maintain the results of the revolution, but this connection proved to be fateful. The "victorious destruction" prevailed, which halted and destroyed the revolutionary process that had been the condition of a transition to communism. According to Badiou, the history of the USSR is a historical demonstration of this problem. The Leninist party was inadequate to the tasks that the transition to communism presented before it, even though its political form had been suitable for leading the party to a victorious uprising. Badiou then sees the Chinese Cultural Revolution as an attempt to resolve this problem—however, its results were ambiguous. While it's true that the revolutionary process was renewed, it was not connected with sufficiently effective organizational forms.[9] In *Theory of the Subject*, Badiou openly writes about the crisis of Marxism as a certain type of politics and he formulates new starting points, methodological approaches, and conceptions, out of which his three-part opus magnum has grown: the books *Being and Event*, *Logics of Worlds*, and *The Immanence of Truths*.[10] At the end of the 1970s, Badiou realized the deep and perhaps final crisis of Marxism as an emancipatory type of politics that, after 1917, had initiated radical political events as well as their consequences. In the 1970s, Marxist politics had become an "oppressive and fragmentary assemblage of ideas and behaviors, captured in a labyrinth of debris and survivors."[11]

Badiou later sees this crisis of Marxism as the end of the sequence of the idea of communism connected with the state as a structure of representation. In *Theory of the Subject*, he wrote about the end of the three referents of Marxist politics. The state referent, which was the actual existence of "Marxist states," disappears as an emblem of the possible victory of Marxist politics. The second disappearing referent is national liberation movements as another emblem of Marxist politics in which there was "the fusion of the national principle and the popular principle." The third disappearing referent is the workers' movements, especially their incarnations in "working-class parties" that were "mixed figures of a distant revolutionary Idea and the proximity of an oppositional activity."[12] In this way, Badiou expresses the collapse of Marxism as historically specific revolutionary thinking and politics. As he says, it is impossible for Marxism to deduce anything that is significant for the present from its recent past. "Its credit has run out."[13] According to Badiou, we should "expatriate" Marxism from theory and politics because it has already lost its historical home. All political referents connected with a worker and popular life are, "with regard to Marxism, atypical, delocalised, errant."[14] At this time, Badiou developed a form of argumentation that emphasized "expatriating Marxism," and de facto called for detaching from Marxist politics that developed the "state idea of communism." From the perspective of *Being and Event*, *Logics of Worlds*, and *The Immanence of Truths*, "expatriating Marxism" means emigrating from the state type of politics that had created the communist sequence of the twentieth century that had closed.

The end of the communist sequence raises a question that is crucial for situating Badiou's philosophy in the interregnum. In Badiou's works, we only find a clear answer in *The Immanence of Truths*, and not earlier. If the event sequence disappears, as is the case with Marxist politics, is it necessary to renounce fidelity to an event whose historical epoch has closed? Toula Nicolacopoulos and George Vassilacopoulos pose the question of what fidelity to an event consists of in the time of its retreat when the revolutionary project is collapsing. Doesn't this situation, which corresponds to the end of the Marxist historical epoch, invite unfaithfulness to the event that gave rise to Marxist politics? These authors claim that in the theory of the event, Badiou did not elaborate a conception of the retreat of the event and had instead dealt with the subject of fidelity only in relation to the occurrence of an event.[15] Their finding may be due to the fact that in his work, Badiou primarily focuses on the existence of truths, which is a question of paramount importance for him. However, the need to disengage from the Marxist sequence is quite adequately demonstrated by Badiou's theory of the disappearance of the three referents of Marxist politics and the subsequent expatriation of Marxism from emancipatory theory and politics. We can ask what is the case with fidelity to an event in the situation of an interregnum—that is, after the end of the event sequence. If the subject were to remain faithful to an event whose sequence has ended, what kind of subject is this?

Badiou's writing only offers clues about the topic of fidelity after the end of a historical sequence that a subject has remained faithful to. Nevertheless, it is possible to assume that this subject doesn't correspond to Badiou's understanding of the loyal subject. It follows that fidelity to an event in the situation of an interregnum does not consist in maintaining a sequence whose historical epoch has ended. As will be discussed later, Badiou defines the faithful subject by its performing operations of fidelity that connect certain elements of the present to the event. These operations create political subjects, such as Leninist parties or national liberation movements. If this sequence runs into a dead end, as was the case with Leninist parties connected to a state, it means that the faithful subject cannot continue within this sequence. The faithful operation ends because, in the dead end, the subject cannot find any more elements that they can connect to the event, which here was the October Revolution. This event had sequences that failed to solve the problem inscribed into itself; that is, according to Badiou, the contradiction between the revolutionary process and the state. What would continuing in fidelity to a politics whose historical sequence had closed this way mean?

We can take the "hard-core communists" as an example. Let's say that this is a group that is faithful to the politics and theory that made up the historically closed sequence in which its fundamental contradiction was never resolved. If the hard-core communists attempt to undertake a faithful operation and connect to the events of the October Revolution—for example, as the alter-globalization movement from the turn of the millennium did—this operation will founder because the state-party, as a referent or subject of this fidelity, after a certain historical point, was suppressing the communist truth procedure connected with equality (according to Badiou, this deadening point arrived with the rise of Stalin in the Soviet Union, or a little later, in China with the end of the Cultural Revolution). We encounter this phenomenon in another form in the orthodox Trotskyite organizations, such as the Socialist Organization of Working People [Socialistická organizace pracujících] or the Revolutionary Communist League (International) RCL(I), which in the 1990s was directly following the conceptions and slogans that Trotsky created in the 1930s and 1940s and summarized in the "Transitional Program for the IV. International." It was an attempt at an "authentic" follow-up to the event of the October Revolution and the first stage of its sequence (Lenin and Trotsky), which Stalin had suppressed when he imposed the form of a "degenerated workers' state" upon it. Even in this case, the connection of elements of the present time to this event and the continuation of the sequence of the faithful subject could not take place. There has been a permanent disconnect inserted between Trotskyism and elements of the present, such as the alter-globalization movement, which makes it evident that the event sequence that began with the October Revolution is historically closed and it is no longer possible to continue within it.

I have done this analysis here in order to clearly demonstrate that fidelity to an event during the period of the interregnum, the way Badiou has it in mind, is fidelity of another kind than continuing in an event sequence that has been historically closed. It follows from Badiou's words about the expatriation of Marxism and a new beginning for philosophy that it is essential to establish a dividing line between the subject and a past event sequence. Badiou expresses himself clearly on this matter: he argues that Marxism, the workers' movement, mass democracy, Leninism, the proletarian parties, and the Soviet state are all lacking any kind of practical significance today, even though they are "remarkable inventions of the twentieth century."[16] He confirms this separation from the previous communist sequence with the words: "what will come will not be, and cannot be, a continuation of the second sequence . . . the second sequence is closed, and it is no good trying to continue or restore it."[17] In *Manifesto for Philosophy*, Badiou considers the Cultural Revolution, May 1968, the Solidarity movement, and other events from the years 1965–80 as unique, though ambiguous events. In the books *The Meaning of Sarkozy* and *The Communist Hypothesis*, he emphasizes that these events belong to a closed sequence and "this is why our research is so complicated, so erratic, so experimental."[18] According to Badiou, the results of the events of May 1968 were amorphous, and the Chinese Cultural Revolution caused a decade of chaos. I presented Badiou's understanding of these events and political experiments in more detail in the introductory section of this book. It's clear from his own statements that he does not believe we can directly follow up on these events and experiments and be "faithful" to them in the sense of a subject who develops their truth procedure. Badiou draws a dividing line between these events and experiments and our situation. For Badiou, the Chinese Cultural Revolution as politics without a state is merely a starting point for seeking new forms of the communist hypothesis, just as the Paris Commune at the end of the first sequence was the starting point for Lenin and for Rosa Luxemburg.[19] It should be added that at that time there was also a division between the situation where Lenin and Luxemburg were acting and the Paris Commune, and it was an interval period between the first and second sequences of the communist idea. Badiou's statements about political and social movements and uprisings starting in the late 1960s (the first period of the Iranian Revolution—the uprising against the Shah, the Political Organization in France, the Zapatista movement in Mexico, the Maoists in Nepal, the Arab Spring, etc.)[20] According to Badiou, these movements and uprisings do not belong to the communist sequence of the twentieth century but are instead part of the interval period, as follows from his assessment of the Arab Spring of 2011–12, in which he sees the first wave of a global human uprising against the worldwide regression caused by the unlimited rule of a financial and imperial oligarchy, the link between parliamentarianism and capital, economic and political authoritarianism, and exploitation. In Badiou's view, this wave is blind, naïve, fragmented, and lacking in standardized conceptions or permanent organization. It is thus reminiscent of the first uprising of the working class in the nineteenth century. Badiou considers this wave of street riots as the beginning of a "return of history" that will bring global resistance to the above-named phenomena and create conditions for a new modification of the communist idea.[21] This first wave of awakened history gives rise to the awareness that it is necessary to dream again because what has been dreamed can, in principle, be realized. According to what Badiou claims, dreaming prevents us from falling into the nihilistic notion that the future does not exist, and it enables us to "go through the painful years of an intervallic period."[22]

These movements and uprisings have not created the truth procedures that Badiou associates with the faithful operation and the political subject. Therefore, it can be argued that in this sense the political truth procedures are not present in our time. The political and social movements and uprisings that appeared at the end of the communist sequence are merely an emerging fragment of the faithful subject, because they lack many of the qualities that Badiou attributes to the faithful subject, such as a political conception, a name, and a development of faithful operations. We discover that the relationship between philosophy and political truth is not a conditioning relationship, but there is a caesura between them. In the interval period or in the interregnum, political truth does not condition philosophy in a direct manner, so the position of philosophy will differ from the position Badiou assigns it in *Manifesto for Philosophy*.

The Closing of Artistic Truths

The case is the same with artistic truths as with political truths in the interregnum. Here, too, we discover the caesura between the contemporary situation and artistic truths in the past. The artistic truths seem to be ongoing generic procedures, and they condition philosophy. Badiou confirms their existence in *Handbook of Inaesthetics*, where he says that "there are artistic configurations, there are works that constitute the thinking subjects of these configurations"—and there is philosophy, which conceptually separates their truths from mere opinion.[23] In the same book, he then identifies the presence of these artistic truths in poetry, theater, film, and dance. The main reference points he uses are Mallarmé and Pessoa.

In "Third Sketch of a Manifesto of Affirmationist Art," artistic truths take on a new character because here Badiou bases his approach on the situation in contemporary art. The features of contemporary artistic production that he calls postmodern provide evidence for the absence of generic procedures in contemporary art. In the ideas and creations of contemporary artists, he sees a "spectacular exhibition of desires, of phantasy, and of terror," which are exhibited as total particularisms and the "historical equality of formal means."[24] The endless domination of particularity and multiplicity has abolished every universality and established an equality of formal means. Badiou's words are uncompromising and sometimes sarcastic when addressing the situation in contemporary art. It soon becomes quite clear that this state in art must be rejected and it's necessary to create the intellectual conditions for art to make a new beginning marked by truths. "We should oppose all those who want only to terminate, the entire cohort of last men, exhausted and parasitical, and their infernal 'modesty'. The end of art, of metaphysics, of representation, of imitation, of transcendence, of the work, of the spirit . . . Enough! Let's proclaim at a stroke an end to all ends, and the possible beginning of all that is, as of all that was, and will be."[25] In art, it is necessary to proclaim the existence of "something that, for the poor century now under way, no longer exists: monumental construction, projects, the creative force of the weak, the overthrow of established powers."[26] It is evident that Badiou considers this artistic production, which no longer even speculates on the existence of any truths, to be so widespread that it has lent contemporary art as a whole a unifying name of "postmodern" that refers to the characteristics described above. Tellingly, with only a few exceptions (e.g., Wim Wenders's films mentioned in the *Handbook of Inaesthetics*), he identifies truths as generic procedures in the works of artists who belong to either the recent or more distant history of art. In his "Third Sketch of a Manifesto of Affirmationist Art," he names Pessoa, Celan, Mandelstam, and Stevens in poetry, Picasso in painting, Schönberg in music, Brecht in theater, Zadkine in sculpture, Chaplin in film, Faulkner in novels, and Cunningham in dance. The very need to express one's attitude toward art as "Third Sketch of a Manifesto of Affirmationist Art" also makes it quite clear that conditioning philosophy with artistic truths isn't conditioning philosophy with contemporary art. The proclamation of affirmationism represents an act of intervention by philosophy into the contemporary state of art. Badiou believes that it is necessary to re-establish affirmative art as art that affirms the existence of truths, and thus it is an expression of the possibility that exists for *future* art.

Let us take note of the subsequent interpretation of the qualities that Badiou attributes to artistic truths in "Third Sketch of a Manifesto of Affirmationist Art." It focuses on these qualities in their identification: incorporeal rigor, anti-romantic coldness, the subtractive operations by which art holds most tightly to imageless real.[27] The artistic truths in the twentieth century are distinguished by "the same impersonal rigour as that of mathematics."[28] Badiou shares the statement by Alvaro de Campos (Pessoa's heteronym) as an emblem of these truths: "Newton's binomial is as beautiful as the Venus de Milo."[29] "Subtraction" of phantasms, immediate emotionality, self-expression, and various contexts and non-artistic demands are a method for affirming the universal. As is obvious, Badiou's formulation of these characteristics of artistic truths is based on subtractive operations of mathematical thought. A truth that belongs to another domain than art is operative in his conception of affirmationism as a renewal of art: the truth of mathematics as a generic procedure that enables thinking about universality. Mathematics enables new beginnings in art, as has already happened in the history of art several times. In "Third Sketch of a Manifesto of Affirmationist Art," Badiou writes: "for the struggle against expressiveness, against Romantic formalism, all that there is is the dynamic of abstraction. This rule is a very old one, but it is especially relevant to our situation. Everything comes down to this: to invent a new sensory abstraction. It is true that we barely know how. Scientific practice, at least, or especially mathematics, can instruct us. After all, this is the path that was taken by people during the Renaissance, and also by painters at the beginning of the twentieth century: they turned to geometry. And we should also turn to geometry, which has changed a great deal."[30]

It's clear from this quotation that Badiou considers the contemporary situation in art to be analogous to the situation before the arrival of the Renaissance or before the birth of modern art. Mathematics, in the form of geometry, should be a guide to proceeding in art so that new forms of artistic truths can emerge. However, we are not going to find these truths in contemporary art if we don't count certain signs that Badiou mentions only in passing. In the book *The Immanence of Truths*, he considers certain dialectics in cinema and "its offspring, television and the internet." Undoubtedly, these media are part of the "artistic-industrial complex of Capital," but at the same time due to the truth procedure in them that is inscribed into the very medium of film, works are created that take aim against the contemporary form of politics and society. Badiou cites the example of a critical documentary or the genre called docufiction in which certain hard-hitting research, which is often undertaken blindly, captures both the reality of life among regular people and activists and also the structures exposed to oppression.[31] As an example of this hard-hitting research in Czech documentaries, we can turn to the work of Karel Vachek, particularly his *Communism and the Net or the End of Representative Democracy* (2019), in which he organically connects the postmodern decentered or rhizomic imagination, critical thinking about the contemporary world, and illustration of the political truth procedure of the Prague Spring of 1968.

I have provided characteristics of the cultural and artistic formations of the present stage of the interregnum discussed at the end of Part One of the book, and in critical documentaries and in docufiction, we encounter a circulation between the pole of postmodern multiplicity, decentralization, and the networking of meanings and the pole of the renewal of artistic truths. According to my classification, Badiou here provides an example of a formation in which pre-evental circulation is taking place. In *The Immanence of Truths*, he expands his investigation of artistic truth procedures when he addresses their "objective" existence in individual artistic genres. This is why he also speaks of truth procedures in the genres of visual art, whose very nature makes it impossible for them to take on the qualities that Badiou in the "Manifesto of Affirmationism" attributes to artistic truths, such as the greatest possible proximity to truth without the use of images. If Badiou finds the truth procedure in the documentary genre, this procedure in principle is also possible to ascribe to contemporary expressions of artistic realism, such as radical realism and certain forms of Stuckism, even though these artistic trends do not have the creation of abstract works as their goal. The truth procedures in critical documentaries, docufiction, or other genres are part of a certain dialectic or circulation between poles that prevent them from taking on the qualities of truth procedures, such as the retroactive naming of an event with which faithful operations (etc.) have been associated.

These statements by Badiou on contemporary art show that artistic truths as generic procedures developed by living artists have closed, as testified in his selection of examples from modern art. However, a new form of these artistic truths has not yet emerged, or it still has a merely dialectical or circulatory nature that in the metamodernist vocabulary expresses a will to the renewal of truths while also ironizing them as soon as this will becomes too specific and too strong. Badiou argues that artistic truths have ceased to operate in contemporary art as living and full-fledged generic procedures; however, full-fledged new procedures have not yet been fully developed. "Postmodern art" in his view shows signs of the interregnum, so contemporary art belongs in an interval period or an interregnum. The truth procedures of contemporary art, if any exist at all, are so weak that they cannot condition philosophy.

Closing the Truth of Love

In *Manifesto for Philosophy*, Badiou writes that philosophy is also conditioned by the truth procedures of love. He cites Jacques Lacan's psychoanalytical discoveries and takes them as the starting point for his theory of love. In the book *In Praise of Love*, Badiou cites Rimbaud's direction that "love needs re-inventing."[32] It then shows that truth procedures do not appear in today's prevailing understanding of intimate relationships. According to Badiou, there are two dominant conceptions of love. One is love as a contractual relationship, and the other is love as desire. In the first case, two individuals enter into a contract on the basis of each one's considerations of what the other person can offer them. The relationship as a contract is based on an exchange between two people who have counted all the pros and cons and considered the other person's value according to various criteria such as sexual attractiveness, hobbies, horoscopes, education, social contacts, and property. Badiou writes about the internet dating agency Meetic, which offers introductions with a minimal risk of becoming inappropriately emotionally involved. This agency arranges acquaintance without the risk that one will experience the torments of love and act against their own interests. It's a love without risk, where as many parameters in selecting the "best partner" are calculated as possible.[33] Badiou combines this concept of love with a liberal right-wing conception of interpersonal relationships as contracts between two individuals who are pursuing their own interests.[34] Let us add that this service in the field of interpersonal relationships imitates the "best practices" used by the management of today's corporations, as discussed above. A person is under a certain degree of psychological pressure in choosing an approach to selecting a partner that will bring them the "best" possible one. This "best practice" in the field of love poses the question to this individual of why not use this practice? Don't they want the "best" for themselves? It's a similar question that leads corporations to implement the "best practices." The right liberal conception of love as a contract assumes that individuals behave like self-investing human capital that invests its time, emotions, and money into a partner relationship and expects that the investment will pay off. It's a concept of the relationship that arises between two neoliberal subjects. In the subchapter on the neoliberal subject in Part One of the book, we have seen that this subject splits internally in the period of the crisis of neoliberalism that arrived after the financial crisis of 2008. At this point, the requirement for self-sacrifice appears, and this overcomes self-interest. There is a certain conservative transformation in self-investing human capital that takes place in connection with the neoliberal demand for self-sacrifice on behalf of the whole economy. There is a tear in the contract between neoliberal subjects that is caused by them being fractured (split between self-interest and self-sacrificing). This tear in the right liberal conception of a relationship can explain the fact that "family values" and self-sacrificing for one's family is a conservative political motif that appeals to a fairly large part of society.

An equally widespread conception of love, Badiou says, is the liberal left-wing vision of fulfilling sexual desires in diverse ways. This approach expresses individuals' democratic right to sexual satisfaction. This approach prioritizes individuals' longings over the commitments and limitations that arise from their social ties. Badiou comments that love, as the satisfaction of an individual's desire, leads to this right being fulfilled by pornography, which has become one of the world's largest industries.[35] In his book *The Pornographic Age*, he writes about the extraordinary position in contemporary democracy, which he approaches in this work from political and ontological perspectives.[36] From the perspective of politics, contemporary democracy is a system of capitalo-parliamentarism where the rule of law (a constitution) and the plurality of parliamentary parties are accompanied by the needs of capital. Thus, the real politics that used to be a struggle between conceptions of society has disappeared and the activities of the parties consist in serving this economic power, which Badiou describes as a kind of prostitution.[37] From the perspective of ontology, Badiou conceives of democracy in such a way that the individual formed by the contemporary world acknowledges only the objective existence of bodies and the multiplicity of communities, sexual and cultural identities, and customs, which he considers to all be equal. Everything deserves to be protected by the law because these "languages" are connected with the life of bodies. A social consensus that only a multiplicity of bodies associated with a multiplicity of languages objectively exist is called democratic materialism. According to Badiou, democratic materialism is characterized by not recognizing the existence of truths and by granting equalities to the language that doesn't acknowledge the normative equality of other languages.[38]

Badiou here indirectly touches upon the antinomy of the postmodern left, which assigns equality to all cultures and is therefore required to consider Enlightenment culture with its universal human rights as just as equal as the rest. Alain de Benoist and the Identitarian movement make the same claim, and they come to the logical conclusion that it isn't possible to criticize the ethical customs of other cultures, such as female genital mutilation, in the name of human rights because this is only the expression of one particular culture. Although Badiou did not deal with democratic materialism from the perspective of its antinomy, it is possible to postulate that its materialist dialectics, which recognize the existence of bodies, languages, and, besides these, also the existence of truths, enable this antinomy. Political analysts are aware that the Identitarian movement or postmodern neofascism takes advantage of this antinomy, and they therefore propose a return to the universalism of human rights or to a new connection between difference and universalism, which Miranda Christou considers the main challenge that postmodern fascism has brought forward, as was discussed in the subchapter "The Identitarian mutation of postmodernism." Badiou avoids the trap of human rights universalism, which is that the culture perceives it as a unification of its diversity and then rejects this concept as a form of Eurocentric violence (see Deleuze's critique of human rights, provided in the previously mentioned subchapter). He pits the universality of truths against the unifying universalism of human rights. He understands them as procedures that do not disturb the elements of culture in every local place but instead give them a new meaning because it either does or doesn't connect them to the event. Badiou's conceptions of truths as a response to sophisticated postmodern fascism are still awaiting a theoretical elaboration.

We have explained Badiou's conception of democracy so that we can better recognize the relationship between the liberal right conception of love as a contract and the liberal left conception of love as desire. Their relationship is indicated in the dense thread of the brief text of *The Pornographic Age*, in which Badiou writes about pornography as the dominant form of image production, which ensures the continuation of democracy in the sense of capitalo-parliamentarism and democratic materialism. Pornographic image production acts as the main ideology of the present time. According to Badiou, within its obscene images there is a connection of "the potentially sophisticated arousal of a desire with the vulgarity of commercial propaganda,"[39] and not only at the level of sexual desire but also at the political and cultural levels. The left liberal conception of love as desire and the right liberal understanding of love as contracts are brought together in pornography. Obscene pictures arouse and then satisfy the liberal individualistic type of desire, which is distinguished by its short duration, flexibility, and promiscuity, which passes between the objects of desire in the same way that we move "from one model of car to another."[40] The right liberal conception of love as contracts here takes on the form of contracts between the consumer of pornography and the person who exhibits their body and their (feigned) excitement in the pornography industry. The claim can be made that the pornography industry is similar to dating agencies like Meetic, even though Badiou himself does not draw this parallel. However, if we are going to develop Badiou's compendious ideas shared in *The Pornographic Age*, we'll then see that the pornography industry promises clients that it provides them with "sex without the risks of sex," in a similar way that Meetic offers "love without love." The pornographic image industry is a source of practices that are used by agencies like Meetic because both of the latter encourage a similar kind of exposure when arranging encounters as the pornographic industry, which represents the dominant form of imagination. It's an expose that in a certain sense represents the culmination or extension of pornographic obscenity, because it doesn't only concern sexual questions, but also all the other sides of clients' lives. The difference between the pornography industry and the Meetic agency is that in the pornographic industry there is an exploitation of the person who is exhibited. The pornography industry is one of the most profitable branches of contemporary digital capitalism, whose products are the most-watched genre on the internet. The left liberal right of the individual to satisfy their desire is fulfilled in pornography, which offers this desire an obscene object of an exhibited body and its expressions. At the same time, this object is also part of the pornographic industry on the basis of the right liberal understanding of a "contract" in which it is being exploited. The desire for a body that has the character of a commodity is aroused by the capitalism of obscene images, in a similar way that the labor force of the proletariat is a commodity in Marx's analysis of capitalism. The connection of the left liberal and right liberal conception of love in its most sophisticated form takes place right at this point. Desire is satisfied by the image of a body that has the nature of a commodity and is the object of exploitation. The pleasure involved is derived from an exploited body whose exploitation is obscured by its obscene image. The left liberal right to satisfaction is fulfilled on the basis of a liberal right "contract" that legalizes the exploitation of this body by the pornography industry. If there were a demand for the abolition of exploitation, including exploitation by the pornography industry, the left liberal conception would mean abolishing the individual right to satisfy desire.

Let's return now from this expansion of Badiou's ideas to what he actually states in *The Pornographic Age*. Here, as his reference point Badiou uses Jean Genet's *The Balcony*, which is set in a brothel—a place where obscenity is part of its order, and this order offers satisfaction of desire for money.[41] In Badiou's view, a brothel is an order that, in his terminology, is a "state" (*état*),[42] in which love has turned into a marketable obscenity that arouses and fulfills desire. The brothel is what best characterizes democracy in the sense of capitalo-parliamentarism and democratic materialism. Democracy as capitalo-parliamentarism is an order or state with its laws, elections, and mechanisms that are inseparable from the capitalist exchange of commodities. The obscenity of the body in a brothel corresponds to the role pornography plays for democracy in the sense of democratic materialism, which acknowledges only the objective existence of bodies and a multiplicity of languages (cultural and sexual identities, customs, etc.). The body and its sexual gratification are what, in democratic materialism, create the basic right that pornography fills as the unifying source of imagery when preserving a multiplicity of languages. Democratic materialism leads to the formation of desire through pornographic imagery. It impresses a certain form onto the various types of desire so that their satisfaction is accomplished through procedures that take place in capitalo-parliamentarism. Let us recall the photographs of the former Czech prime minister and liberal-conservative politician Mirek Topolánek, which were taken when he was taking part in a sophisticated erotic soiree organized by Silvio Berlusconi. "Democratic" desire is formed pornographically, and the images of naked top politicians fulfill this desire. This doesn't only have to concern obscene photographs; it can also involve exposing details from their private lives, according to the template in tabloid magazines. Democratic materialism is linked to the brothel of capitalo-parliamentarism by converting the individual to a mere body and granting it the right to satisfy its desire. However, this is a desire modeled according to the obscene depictions produced by the pornography industry. Pornographic desire legitimizes capitalo-parliamentarism as a brothel. According to Badiou's interpretation of Genet's play *The Balcony*, the brothel embodies capitalo-parliamentarism as an order or state that satisfies cultural and political desires formed by the pornography industry on the basis of exchange. I have deduced from Badiou's reflections on this topic that democratic materialism can be understood as the ontological condition of capitalo-parliamentarism.

I have expanded upon Badiou's condensed and perhaps even too-succinct text in the book *The Pornographic Age* in order to make it clear that if Badiou speaks of the need to reinvent love, it's not just a conception of love that will be in opposition to the dominant forms of love such as individual desire and contractual relationships. In *The Pornographic Age*, Badiou finds that the forms of "love without love" have a much more significant social import than he attributed to them in previous works. They do not only concern the relationship between two individuals, but in the form of pornography, they are also interrelated with the contemporary state, which is capitalo-parliamentarism. In Badiou's view, the generic procedure of love differs in many regards from the left liberal conception of love as desire and from the right liberal understanding of love as contracts. An event encounter by two people cannot be calculated in the same way as dating agencies such as Meetic: it is a random encounter that is surprising and disconcerting, which foils calculations and considerations of their benefits.[43] The meeting event, which is the beginning of love, is in itself opaque. It is only named as an event in hindsight, which corresponds to Badiou's general conception of the event. Already, this evental nature of the encounter is in contradiction with the conception of love as a contract that arises as an agreement between two individuals who prudently pursue their own interests. According to Badiou, the crucial factor is the generic love procedure, which is subsequent to this encounter. Love happens at the "Two scene," which maintains the infinite difference of both people.[44] However, the permanent separation of the lovers as individuals differs fundamentally from the liberal understanding of love as the purposeful union of two individuals. According to Badiou, the relationship between me and another person arises and is maintained because I look at the world through the perspective of the other, who is different from me. The other is a decentered point of view for me, which is different from the perspective of my self-interest and a narcissistic confirmation of my identity.[45] The crucial quality of love is that I experience the world from the perspective of two instead of one. This happens, for example, "when I lean on the shoulder of the woman I love, and can see, let's say, the peace of twilight over a mountain landscape, gold-green fields, the shadow of trees, black-nosed sheep motionless behind hedges and the sun about to disappear behind craggy peaks, and know—not from the expression on her face, but from within the world as it is—that the woman I love is seeing the same world, and that this convergence is part of the world and that love constitutes precisely, at that very moment, the paradox of an identical difference, then love exists, and promises to continue to exist."[46] The difference between two people as a nearly infinite number of different qualities, thoughts, ideas, and memories is a condition for the further development of this experience of the world together.

The truth procedure of love consists in "building" the shared world, which is no longer a mere experiencing of the magic power of the first encounters, in which the romantic conception of love remains absorbed. Building a shared world for two requires persistence over time. Without perseverance and a certain tenacity, the shared world will fall apart and the "identical difference" of love disappears. The truth procedure of love has the nature of enduring fidelity, which enables it to "triumph" over obstacles that arise in the world. Love is not just an emotional state, but the building of a world that is impossible over the long term without a certain discipline of fidelity, which, however, represents an adventure.[47] Loyalty presupposes that the individual is able to prioritize the shared perspective over the perspective of private self-interest. Liberal individualism as an adherence to self-interest is thus that which is in conflict with the development of love as the building of a shared world. Badiou calls the preference of the shared over the individual the communist element of love and he proposes a further definition: love is minimal communism.[48] Badiou argues with a certain Christian author, who claims that a child is the fulfillment of love, and the goal of love is thus the number three. Badiou sees in the child a certain turning point in the relationship, which often causes new decisions that are made from the perspective of a certain repetition of the evental encounter at the beginning of the love affair. However, he refuses to claim that a child is the condition of the fulfillment of love because this would deny the possibility of building a shared world, and therefore the truth of love for childless couples, homosexuals, and other types of relationships that do not produce children.[49] Badiou conceives of the family as a state of love, which acts similarly to the state in the domain of political truths. It creates a structure where there is the threat that love will cease to be creative and will no longer develop as a truth procedure. Instead of "Scene Two," where the identical difference emerges, a tendency toward ownership and egoism develops within the family as a state. The goal of love is not to reproduce the family, but to experience the world from the perspective of difference. However, family or marriage integrates the love relationship into society, which gives love a certain social form. According to Badiou, love is difficult to maintain in a given society without this social form. He compares the truth procedure of love to the truth procedure of politics, which "probably can never be accomplished entirely without the state."[50]

In this revelation in Badiou's "invention" of love, we see that love, as a truth procedure, is in contradiction with both of the dominant conceptions of love in the present time. It contradicts the right liberal conversion of love to a contract between two prudent individuals pursuing their own interests. The encounter event contradicts calculations about the benefits of living with the other, and the relationship of love expresses a prioritization of the other. Love is also at odds with the left liberal understanding of love as an individual's fulfillment of their desires. The truth procedure, as the building of one world from the perspective of difference, assumes that the fulfillment of an individual's desire and their narcissism will be subordinated to the shared work of love, in which a certain infinite dimension appears, as Badiou writes in *The Immanence of Truths*.[51] Love contains this "minimal communism," which changes the relationship to one's own desire and incorporates it into "Scene Two." Badiou's understanding of love also runs counter to conservatism, which subordinates love to the commitments and responsibilities that arise from marriage and the family as the higher sense of love. The conservative goal of love (a child and reproduction of society) leads to homosexuals and other sexual identities being denied the right to marriage. Badiou rejects this conservative attitude toward sexual minorities because he doesn't believe that a child or the reproductive function is the goal of love. Childless marriages that don't fulfill the reproductive function have the same significance as marriages with children if they are a place where love's truth procedure is taking place.

It's clear from Badiou's approach, which focuses on the reinvention of love, that love doesn't exist as a truth procedure in such a form that it could condition philosophy, as he writes in *Manifesto for Philosophy*. It is certainly not the case that love has ceased to exist as a phenomenon of interpersonal relations. As we have seen in the subchapter "The domain of cultural theory: fiduciary realism, monism, and the affective turn," contemporary cultural theorists are discovering the subject of love in today's literature, in which Barthes's understanding of love as a cultural construct is ironized, for example, in Eugenides's novel *The Marriage Plot*. Badiou's theory of love can be understood as the conceptual representation of relationships that appear after the end of postmodernism.

The dominant forms of love are love as a contract and love as individualistic desire. As demonstrated in Badiou's text *The Pornographic Age*, these two conceptions are not merely a matter of a certain lifestyle or personal preferences, but they are connected with democracy in the sense of capitalo-parliamentarism and democracy, meaning democratic materialism. These conceptions of love are intertwined with pornography, which is the industrial branch that produces the dominant form of imagery, which is obscenity. Based on Badiou's reasoning, we can claim that both conceptions of love are realized not only as the result of a personal decision but also forms that condition the further continuation of the given political and economic system at the level of interpersonal relations. These are two interconnected types of love, which are ideological forms of capitalo-parliamentarism. This aspect reveals two facts. First, the phenomenon of love, which corresponds to the truth procedure, is difficult to represent in a world in which the right liberal and left liberal conceptions of love predominate. However, the second fact is of greater importance: the phenomenon of love is in contradiction with these two dominant conceptions of interpersonal relations, and these conceptions make up the ideological forms of capitalo-parliamentarism. The phenomenon of love that Badiou "discovers" is thus in contradiction with the ideological forms of interpersonal relations embodied in pornography. Therefore, it can be argued that the phenomenon of love lacks a sufficient place allocated for it in contemporary society in order to function as a truth procedure. Love as fidelity, perseverance, and building a shared world represents a procedure that disrupts the contemporary ideology of interpersonal relations. Its social place is a non-place.

In *The Pornographic Age*, Badiou used formulations that perhaps better than any of his other expressions indicate that he conceives of the interval period as an interregnum, as was discussed at the beginning of this book: "the old beauty is no longer beautiful and the new truth is not yet true"; "the old revolutionary politics is no longer active, and where the new politics is, with difficulty, experimenting with its truth." The same is true for the form of love. Its old forms are no longer active, and the new ones are only now being invented. Badiou's motto itself, that it's necessary to reinvent love, is eloquent enough. If love conditions philosophy as a truth procedure, it is not a form of love that currently exists in a represented form in the present time. It is only possible to consider fragments of its representation, as in Eugenides's novel *The Marriage Plot*, which was mentioned above. Badiou refers to countless examples in literature, in which we discover experiences and dramas that express an encounter as an event and a truth procedure, but they are literary works of the past (such as Shakespeare's tragedy *Romeo and Juliet*).[52] Badiou does not situate the truth procedures of love in the interval or interregnum, but rather in the past and also in the future, so long as love can be rediscovered in such a way that it becomes a represented form of interpersonal relations that creates a dividing line between itself and the ideological forms of love. The truth procedure of love, as it existed in the past, is closed, and therefore there is a caesura between it and the current situation. For even the truth of love cannot condition philosophy in the way described in *Manifesto for Philosophy*.

The Demise of Unifying Procedures and the Domination of Multiplicity in the Interregnum

The crucial question was whether there are still truth procedures in today's world as external conditions that enable the existence of philosophy. We have seen that in this form there is no political truth procedure, nor are there truth procedures for art or love. A caesura has appeared before us, which separates these procedures from the contemporary world because their previous forms have all closed and their new forms have not yet been shaped. We only encounter fragments of their future possible forms that correspond to the phenomenon of circulation in which potentially new experiences and experiments have not yet become more permanent lines of generic procedures.

In the case of political truths, the naming of political events and their subjects has acted as the main unifying element (the October Revolution, the Chinese Cultural Revolution, May 1968, the Leninist party, the Shanghai Commune, etc.). This entire sequence contained a series of divisions and splits, but there nevertheless existed a certain unifying reference point, which was the October Revolution being used as the name of the establishing event of the emancipatory politics of the twentieth century. According to Badiou, this sequence closed because it was unable to resolve the contradiction that had already existed at its inception as an establishing event: the contradiction between the revolutionary process and organization connected with a state, which at first protected the revolution from defeat but later suppressed the revolutionary process itself. After the conclusion of this sequence of this communist idea, a situation occurs in which the name of an event that would become a new common point of reference for emancipatory struggles is missing. In the interval period or the interregnum, there is a reigning multiplicity of names, a multiplicity of themes, and also of forms of struggle (e.g., the alter-globalization movement, the anti-capitalist movement, the movement for sexual minorities' rights, feminist movements, and ecological movements). At the same time, it's impossible to renew the previous common reference because its sequence has closed and every attempt at renewing it fails. A multiplicity thus arises for which a unifying reference point cannot be found, and it's also impossible to create one by, hypothetically, connecting all the multiplicities of the movement into common communication and discussion channels with the goal of unifying them. The unification point only appears in certain negative themes that these movements define themselves against, and their unification is only bound to this negative theme, as was the case with the broad-spectrum political initiative ProAlt that arose in 2010 as a reaction to the restrictive social and cultural policies of the neoliberal Czech government. The interregnum, as the end of the political truth procedure, is a period in which multiplicity dominates as the existential form of emancipatory policies. Perhaps we can discover new, experimental forms of unification in movements of the past decade, such as Indignados or the American socialists who are seeking a way to connect the spontaneity of mass movements and the organizational principle of a party. According to Badiou, the possibility of political unification in the interregnum is connected to the event that cannot be foreseen, and whose truths (i.e., generic procedures) can end earlier than its naming happens.

In modern art, the unifying element has several characteristics, which Badiou says distinguish artistic generic procedures: incorporeal rigor, anti-romantic coldness, the subtractive operations by which art holds most tightly to imageless real. Badiou finds these qualities in works by artists in various genres, such as Pessoa, Celan, Mandelstam, Picasso, Schönberg, and Brecht. In specific works of art and genres, these qualities take on many different forms, but what they have in common is that they arise as affirmations of artistic truths that have their individual establishing events (such as Picasso's and Braque's invention of cubism and Schönberg's creation of dodecaphony). Badiou does not identify any individual artistic event that would establish modern art as a whole. In the artistic world, we don't find any parallel to the establishing event of the October Revolution, which would be the beginning of the entire sequence of modernist truth procedures. Modernism's individual artistic truths show certain commonalities that Badiou characterizes in "Third Sketch of a Manifesto of Affirmationist Art" as a sense for monumental construction, projects, the creative force of the weak, and efforts aimed at overthrowing established powers.

In my research, I limited myself to this basic interpretation of Badiou's conception of artistic truths because my goal was to demonstrate the existence of a dividing line between these truths and contemporary art in the situation of the interregnum. This dividing line appears after the closing of modernist truth procedures, and according to Badiou, it has the result that art becomes a "spectacular exhibition of desires, of fantasy and of terror; and under banner of abolishing the universal, that is, the total exhibition of particularism and the historical equality of formal means."[53] The artistic interregnum is dominated by both multiplicity and particularity, which have not only dissolved every universality but also abolished the awareness of any existence of universality in art. Badiou calls this art postmodernism. It is an art that emerges after the end of modernist truth procedures, which, in maintaining its multiplicity, represents certain unifying forms of experience and creativity that are connected to the naming of their establishing events (cubism, abstraction, dodecaphony, epic theater, etc.). Postmodern art also uses certain unifying names, such as pop art, abstract expressionism, and conceptualism, and Badiou does not address the question of whether there has been an experimental search for new conceptions of artistic truths. In Part One of the book, I introduced postmodern art as still having traces of modernist art's truth procedures, and it only later transformed into the kind of postmodern art that Badiou writes about. Certain unifying names, such as conceptualism, can be understood precisely as the presence of a modernist element, which was discussed in connection with the epicyclic character of culture in the first phase of the interregnum. In contemporary art, this name has changed to postconceptualism, which indicates that modernist elements have already ceased operating in it. Badiou describes the state of postmodern art after this extinction of peripheral modernist patterns, when the multiplicity, particularism, and fragmentariness have been totalized. Badiou discovers certain experiments with the renewal of artistic truths in contemporary art, but his goal is not to distort the entirety of contemporary art, so he only mentions seemingly at random certain examples where we find an experimental creation of new forms of unity while multiplicity and particularity are also preserved.

In the question of the truth procedure of love, we have traced the dominant forms of interpersonal relations that remain without the social unifying element that would create "Scene Two" from these individualists. In today's world, Badiou's conception of love as a truth procedure only has a fragmentary symbolic representation because it's necessary to reinvent a new form of love, at the level of symbols and artistic representation.

In this way, Badiou explains why a multiplicity that seems inseparably integrated has dominated politics, art, and love for the past few decades. After the closing of the truth procedures, the shared orientation and reference points that had a unifying effect have disappeared. However, they retained the multiplicity (a multiplicity of emancipatory political trends, modernist art trends, etc.) and they were active even when divisions and fracturing occurred in the movements. The events of May 1968 can serve as an example: there were many different political trends with a great number of varying standpoints, but there was also a dominant consensus on a common language of symbols and colors. The unifying color of these protests was red, which signified the common reference point of the October Revolution. As Badiou says, this was the last time in Western Europe when this unifying symbolism was used by a political and social movement. The fracturing, in which the common language of symbols was lost, indicates the extinguishing and closing of the truth procedure. After their closing, an interregnum begins, in which ex definition plurality dominates. It does not contain truth procedures, or they are not sufficiently developed, and therefore shared orientation and reference points and a common name that would have a unifying effect are all missing.

The domination of this multiplicity without a common language in politics, art, and love creates a situation in which philosophy is conditioned by multiplicities that lack unifying elements. Because they have their reference points and names (such as cubism, dodecaphony, abstraction, and modern poetry in art), truth procedures offer philosophy a certain orientation in the multiplicity of elements that are connected with these truth procedures. Philosophy is conditioned by them in such a way that, thanks to these procedures, it discovers certain unifying lines that enable it to orient itself. External truth procedures condition philosophy's ability to orient itself and to create the kinds of relationships to these procedures where there is a mutual possibility of harmonization or "composability" (Badiou). Philosophy relates to concepts that have a general or even a universal meaning in a given procedure. Concepts such as modern poetry have a meaning that is created in the faithful search for elements that belong to this concept and those that, on the contrary, do not belong to it. Philosophy relates to this meaning of the concept of modern poetry, and it orients itself according to dividing and unifying lines. Therefore, it is able to work with general concepts whose meaning arises through the development of an external truth procedure.

In the first phase of the interregnum, when the traces of these procedures became extinct, postmodern philosophy was still relating to crumbling though still operational general concepts such as Marxism, the Enlightenment, and modern Christianity, which Lyotard had called "grand narratives." The meanings of these general terms were then still formed by their truth procedures. As soon as these procedures became extinct and fell apart, the meaning of these concepts was dispersed into many fragments. There are many various conceptions of modern poetry, many avant-gardes, and many conceptions of the Enlightenment, so it's impossible to create a unifying general conception. Postmodern philosophy has lost the conceptions that it had intended to refashion or to define itself against. In the second chapter of Part One of the book, I discussed McGowan's observation that postmodernism was a project with colossal ambitions, which attempted an overall reevaluation of the intellectual structures of Western culture. Postmodern philosophers have struggled to refashion an approach to concepts such as truth, reason, the subject, and the human being. As soon as the truth procedures were extinguished, the general meaning of the terms fell apart into an irreconcilable multiplicity of elements of meaning, and the character of philosophy changed. As McGowan states, instead of a postmodern vision of an overall transformation of culture and politics, contemporary philosophy and cultural theory deal with careful examination of detailed subjects from various non-unified domains. Philosophy does not approximate itself to truths, but to incoherent multiplicities that remained after the breakdown and disappearance of these truths. Approximation to a multiplicity of detailed subjects causes philosophy to lose its ability to think in general concepts, which would lend this multiplicity some unifying features. The loss of the ability to think in general terms manifests in the dissipation and disappearance of the concept of postmodernism, which Steven Connor argues in the last state in the history of postmodernism, as we saw in the subchapter "The end of communism and the periodization of the cultural interregnum." As Connor writes, the concept of postmodernism has become so indeterminate that it has ceased to serve as a unifying concept for particular cultural models. Although there have been general names for the contemporary cultural situation (metamodernism, remodernism, altermodernism, etc.), these names coexist beside one another as an ununified plurality. Based on my development of Badiou's conceptions, I explain this multiplicity of terms for the present period as testimony to the extinction of truth procedures in the domains of politics, art, and love, which brought about a breakdown of the position that cultural theory and philosophy had enabled to create and maintain a unifying general name for the cultural situation in which these domains are found. Without this position, it is essentially impossible to maintain the conception of a "cultural epoch" and create a name for it that will be generally accepted.

Badiou characterizes the present as a "period of disorientation." Philosophy loses its position and ceases to seek exceptions or problematize the political status quo, which seems like something natural—thus, it refrains from problematizing "democracy." Frank Ruda argues that the previous truths have been "satiated" and philosophy has lost the truth procedure of communism as a condition for its functioning. Democratic materialism condemns the concept of communism as an expression of undemocratic or even "terrorist" thinking. With the loss of the truth procedure of communism, philosophy loses its position, which now seems impossible or inadmissible to the given order. As Ruda writes, "the condemnation of communism means *simply* condemnation of thought, and thus also of philosophy."[54] In my opinion, philosophy's disorientation is caused by the objective disintegration of philosophy's position in the present interregnum, in which not only political truths have ceased to operate but also artistic truths and the truths of love. I attribute philosophy's disorientation to the breakdown of unifying reference points and the general concepts that arose within these procedures.

Our initial question, of how to explain the position of Badiou's philosophy, thus returns with even greater urgency. What is the position occupied by Badiou's philosophy conditioned by if not by truth procedures that have ceased operating in the present period? Yet again, one of the main mysteries of Badiou's philosophy is its situatedness in an interregnum in which truths do not exist and there are only certain experiments and approaches to new truths. In his book *Being and Event*, Badiou claims that the structure of the situation in and of itself does not provide any truths.[55] At the same time, however, in *Manifesto for Philosophy*, he states that philosophy is conditioned by external truths. From this point of view, it seems that Badiou's philosophy paradoxically arises in a situation in which the conditions for its origination are missing. Badiou's philosophy can give rise to the impression of a certain revelation coming from some other time, and we don't know whether it's from the past or the future. In further interpretation, it then turns out that Badiou's philosophy has at least one condition for its existence around, which is the truth developed in mathematics.

The Existence of Mathematical Truths

Thus far, I have left aside the domain of science because it differs from the others discussed in that Badiou finds a unique event there whose truth procedures can develop even in the interregnum situation. These events took place in set theory in connection with groundbreaking discoveries by Cantor, Gödel, and Cohen. In connection with them, Badiou speaks of an intellectual revolution with fundamental philosophical consequences. Among these discoveries, Paul Cohen's discovery from the 1960s occupies a special place. The "Cohen-event" consists in the creation of a generic set and the introduction of an operation called forcing. According to Badiou, these and other concepts of contemporary mathematics are solved at the level of mathematical formulations of ontological problems left to us by the history of philosophy. Cohen's intellectual revolution enabled philosophy to create a new conception of truth and the subject, and it opened a new chapter in ontological thinking.[56] We may ask why Badiou chose set theory instead of some other mathematical theory. After all, he himself says that set theory isn't either the basic theory of mathematics or the most interesting theory. However, he recognized a place in it that has revolutionary philosophical potential. The task of philosophy is to realize set theory's ontological potential and to develop it further. It would be a misunderstanding if we grasped Badiou's philosophy as a philosophy of mathematics. Badiou uses certain fragments from mathematics in a similar way that Aristotle approached logic, which he considered to be the tool or "organon" of philosophical thinking. Badiou does not arrive with new mathematical proofs, nor does he solve questions posed by contemporary mathematics.[57] It turns to certain fragments of mathematical theory that are hiding meanings that change the understanding of ontology and basic philosophical conceptions such as truth, the subject, and the thing. This hidden ontological potential of mathematics can only be recognized by philosophy, while it remains invisible to mathematics because the latter doesn't usually ask ontological questions. Mathematics creates models and operations; philosophy recognizes and formulates their ontological meaning. Badiou's basic definition of the relationship between mathematics and philosophy states that ontology is mathematics and philosophy is meta-ontology.[58]

Mathematics is the place where the event occurred, which is followed by a truth procedure that continues even in the situation of the interregnum. Unlike the other three types of truths, this is a truth that isn't closed and separated by a caesura. Badiou transfers the basic elements of the event to his philosophy, which, besides the generic set and forcing, also includes axioms, theorems, and other concepts from set theory. Badiou's conception of multiplicity and unity, being, event, truth, and the subject, is permeated by elements he borrowed from this turning point in mathematics. We read in *Being and Event* that "the mathematico-logical revolution of Frege-Cantor sets new orientations for thought."[59] Badiou's philosophy does not fully merge into mathematics but maintains a distance because its issue is the basic concepts of the history of philosophy, and not questions that arise within set theory itself. Mathematics creates axioms and theorems that have a dual meaning from the perspective of philosophy. On the one hand, they belong to mathematics and their meaning is given by the internal context of the mathematical world. However, on the other hand, they also have a broader meaning that exceeds the world of mathematics. The transcendental significance of mathematics (set theory) allows philosophy to create new forms of thinking that fundamentally change the manner in which philosophy can now contemplate being, truth, the subject, and other concepts. This new form of philosophical thinking, conditioned by set theory, departs from the history of philosophy in which thinkers—apart from a few exceptions, such as the ancient Atomists—conceived of being through the mediation of natural language. The properties of being were derived from linguistic categories and syntactical relationships, such as the relationship between the subject and the predicate or the syntactic relation in the conditional sentence. The philosophical categories of essence, accident, cause, purpose, and so on, were derived from these linguistic categories and relations. Philosophy was in thrall to language, which impressed a certain form of thinking upon it that appeared to be natural. Badiou conceives of this captivity of philosophy in language as an idealism that he terms "idealinguistery" (*idéalinguisterie*).[60]

Set theory is based on the irremovable logical incoherence of natural language, which expresses Russell's paradox in that natural language admits such properties as not being an element of itself $\neg (a \in a)$. Zermelo shows that there exists a multiplicity of multiplicities whose expression exceeds the capability of language.[61] The multiplicity of multiplicities does not correspond to the basic ontological notion expressed by Plato and Leibniz that the only things that exist are those that can be expressed as "one thing." The multiplicity of multiplicities is not a formation that can be counted as one, and therefore the sentence "the multiplicity of multiplicities exists" disrupts language as a means of ontological thinking. After abandoning language as its basic means, philosophy joins with mathematics (set theory), which becomes a new means for philosophical thinking. Philosophy thinks through mathematics and thus creates intellectual forms that enable it to significantly transform our understanding of philosophical concepts such as being, truth, the subject, finiteness, and infinity. Badiou does not cling to set theory as the only area of mathematics that has significance for philosophy. The second book of his ontological trilogy, *Logics of Worlds*, is connected with the logical theory of categories that conceives of objects as relations and enables the creation of an objective phenomenology of the appearance of truths in the world. Due to the new definition of relations and the world, Badiou focuses on two fragments of this theory, topos theory and Heyting algebra, which make it possible to measure the degree of equality between two elements of a multiplicity. Through this, Badiou formulates the philosophical concept of the "transcendental," which is a function of the appearance of elements in a given world.[62] In the third part of his ontological trilogy, *The Immanence of Truths*, Badiou connects philosophy with the mathematical theory of the types of infinity in its contemporary form, which is called the "theory of large cardinals."[63] This fragment of mathematics allows philosophy to grasp the relationship between the infinite and the finite anew. Truths exist in the finite world, but they relate to the infinite or the "absolute place," which also exists outside of the individual finite world in which these truths arose. On the basis of large cardinal theory, Badiou has created a form of thinking that is able to express truths such as infinity that exist in certain relations to the finite. By using mathematical theories of the types of infinities, Badiou formulates a new conception of "eternal" ideas, which are truths in the sense of a certain type of infinity, which is the non-constructible infinite (Scott's theorem and Jensen's theorem). However, there also exist "eternal" scientific, political ideas, and eternal ideas of love.

The Eccentric Position of Philosophy in the Interregnum

It is now clear that philosophy is conditioned by truth procedures from mathematics that are also operating in the situation of the interregnum, but it is not conditioned in the same sense by truths from politics, art, and love, which are closed as generic procedures. It is possible that if these truths were not closed and Badiou did not create his philosophy in the situation of the interregnum, he would not bring philosophy closer to mathematics and a certain intellectual revolution, or at the very least a dividing line in the history of philosophical ontology would not have happened. If we look at the present interregnum from this point of view, it appears that the absence of truths in the areas of politics, art, and love has conditioned the recognition of the significance of mathematics. Philosophy draws closer to mathematics, which has led to a new beginning for philosophy.

We thus arrive at a special type of conditioning that occurs in the interregnum situation. Philosophy is conditioned by the *absence* of truths; that is, the absence of three types of truths. This is about conditioning with absent object-causes which represent a special type of causal relationship in which the effect is caused by the fact that the place of the cause is empty. This causality of the absent cause makes philosophical thinking focus on one domain, which suggests that there is a latently present place of a philosophical break. In the other domains (politics, art, love), this place is absent. Simply put, from Badiou's perspective, capitalo-parliamentarism, postmodern art, and pornography don't offer anything that would inspire philosophy. Only mathematics remains. Thanks to it, philosophy creates general categories (the event, truth, the subject, etc.) which provide a unifying perspective for assessing the situation in the individual domains. But in addition to this critical significance, these categories also have a constructive significance, as guidelines for orientation in politics, art, and love, and this, according to my terminology, enables distinctions to be made among individual types of circulations (pre-evental, reactive, and obscure). With this distinction, the intellectual conditions are created for the emergence of events and the initiation of truth procedures in these three domains. General categories created through the influence of truths in one domain (in mathematics) thus have not only a critical significance for evaluating the state of different domains but they also function as an anticipation of future events.

Returning to Badiou's *Manifesto for Philosophy*, we see that the position of philosophy in the present interregnum is still not so far from the individual types of truths. It's a position skewed toward the domain of mathematics, in which it finds places that condition philosophy. Thanks to mathematics, philosophy creates unifying general categories for the event, truth, the subject, and so on, which it can then introduce into the other domains. It acts in them like a metatheoretical unifying principle, but it doesn't disrupt their uniqueness. In a situation of the extinction of political truths, artistic truths, and the truths of love, the eccentric position of philosophy is a condition for us to be able to recognize and name these truths, whether they are mere short-term experiments or truths so generic that they are launching a new period of their historical incarnation.

After situating Badiou in the interregnum in this way, perhaps we have come a little closer to an answer to the opening question that concerned the two theses on the position of his philosophy. The first thesis stated that Badiou's philosophy is found among the interregnum formations which show a circulation between unity and multiplicity, between truth and the impossibility of its full presence, and so on. The second thesis stated that Badiou's philosophy created a new beginning of a "doctrine of truths" and it does not show these circulations. Badiou's philosophy, by its structure, does not belong to the interregnum, but it is found there only because it was created in the conditions of the interregnum in which truths are absent. Now we can clarify that the political and artistic truths and the truth of love are missing, but scientific truth (mathematics) is present.

It seems to be the case that Badiou's philosophy is not among the interregnum formations that show circulations, because thanks to having drawn close to mathematics it created a new manner of thinking about unity, multiplicity, truth, the subject, and other concepts that created poles or focal points in these circulations. There are no elliptical circulations or metamodernist oscillations because their relations are of a different type, which will be discussed in the following chapter.

2

The Philosophical Exodus from the Interregnum

Event, Truth, and the Subject as a Composition of Unity and Multiplicity

The Hypothesis of the Exteriority of Badiou's Philosophy

Badiou's philosophy occupies an eccentric position in the interregnum, which enables it to develop concepts and conceptual compositions that have a different nature than elliptical circulation or metamodernist oscillation. I will demonstrate their novelty in their structure, from the perspective of two concepts: unity and multiplicity. I've chosen these terms because I consider them to be appropriate interpretive coordinates for the investigation of Badiou's philosophy in relation to the interregnum. In cultural theory, the concept of unity is understood as a modernist pattern, whereas the concept of multiplicity acts as a postmodernist pattern. In both the elliptical and metamodernist models, they make up two interconnected poles or focal points that are semantically relatively easy to understand. Already during the investigation of the domains of politics, art, and love during the period when their truths were closing, we could convince ourselves of the quality of these two concepts as evidence (see the subchapter "The disappearance of unifying procedures and the dominance of plurality in the interregnum"). Another reason to choose these interpretive coordinates is that we can find the conceptual duality of unity and multiplicity in many of Badiou's concepts and conceptual compositions. I hypothesize that a new type of unity and multiplicity appears within them, and even though they arose within the interregnum, by their nature they still stand outside of it. Thus, in this sense, Badiou's philosophy is exterior to the interregnum. In this way, I will examine the unity and multiplicity in the fundamental categories of Badiou's philosophy, which are the event, truth, and the subject. It is a hitherto undescribed type of unity and multiplicity. I call them fundamental categories because, according to Badiou's statement, the "event" and its relation to the situation is the basis of his entire philosophical structure.[1] Truth and the subject also belong among these bases. Badiou's other categories can be understood as a development of individual aspects of these fundamental categories. For example, the category of infinity is a development of a specific property that is related to the truth procedure. The category of the world is built on the basis of the concept of the "evental trace," connected with the category of the event, and so on.

The Event and the Radicality of Mathematical Ontology

Badiou conceives of the event as a union of multiplicity and unity, in which both have an ontological meaning that will be necessary to clarify. Badiou defines the event as a multiplicity that is always connected with a certain situation. The event arises on the "evental site," which is always local. There is no evental site as one abstract formula, which would somehow determine from the outside where the places that an event could take place are. The local character of the evental site is caused by this place being where, in relation to a specific historical situation and its structure of representation, which Badiou terms the "state." The event as a plurality and as a unity is tied to the basic ontological operation of count-as-one and the term the multiplicity of multiplicities. Badiou philosophically relates to Zermelo and Fraenkel's formal system (ZF), in which there exist only multiplicities where there is no distinction between objects and groups of objects, nor between elements and sets. Multiplicity is always an element of multiplicities. This formation is inconsistent, and we cannot adequately illustrate it as one. It's a formation that natural language is unable to express.[2] A multiplicity of multiplicities is counted as one, but the operation of counting is, in principle, never adequate to the inconsistent character of this multiplicity. The count-as-one operation creates a "presentation" of the given multiplicity, which consists in the multiplicity becoming *one* multiplicity and thereby gaining its ontological consistency. It is presented as one thing. The situation is then defined as a place of counting, which creates a certain structure of multiplicities presented.[3]

We can approach the concepts of multiplicity and the one using an example that doesn't entirely correspond to the radicality of Badiou's ontology. Imagine a human being before the counting operation. This is a hypothetical idea because, as we will see, according to Badiou, there is no such thing as an "original state" that was here before the counting. With this reservation in mind, let's now consider that before the counting operation, the human being is an inconsistent multiplicity of multiplicities. Its body contains chemical elements that are associated with an infinite number of occurrences of these elements in the cosmos. Its speech is made up of sounds that we can examine from many different angles—phonological, semantic, acoustic—and thus connect them with more and more phenomena. However, it is only the counting operation that creates *one* entity out of this multiplicity and assigns it to the set of human beings. The property of "being human" is not an original quality of a specific entity, but is instead the result of the counting operation in which it becomes one entity that is an element of a certain set within the multiplicity of multiplicities. The radicality of Badiou's ontology is that in reality we can never know the state of the world before the beginning of the counting operation. The example provided relies on multiplicities (the multiplicity of occurrences of chemical elements in the cosmos, etc.) which are themselves the result of certain types of counting (the concept of a "chemical element," of "connection," and "cosmos"). According to Badiou, being is neither one nor many, because both categories are the result of a counting operation. The categories "one" and "many" make up a conceptual pair that arises simultaneously within a single operation. If we say that something is "many," its opposite of "one" immediately appears. The multiplicity of multiplicities as the original state of being is the result of a retroactive transference of the category "multiplicity" into a state that is, in principle, unknowable. Being, in itself, doesn't have any structure.[4] The result of the counting is a certain presence of multiplicities whose basic form is "one" and "many." Through Zermelo's theory of the multiplicity of multiplicities, Badiou formulates a new relationship between unity and multiplicity that is already at a basic ontological level. Nor is classical metaphysics, which at least since Plato has considered the *one* to be the essential characteristic of being, in the right. Nor is the ontology of multiplicity created by Heraclitus and represented by Deleuze, which considers multiplicity as something original, correct. Neither the one nor the multiplicity expresses the original state of being. These categories are an element of natural language, which creates the impression that their structure corresponds to the structure of being. Badiou understands this idea, which is used both in classical metaphysics and in the ontology of multiplicities, as an expression of linguistic idealism.

The concept of a situation represents a certain structure of presented multiplicities. However, there is yet another structuring that arrives, which creates the "representation" of the situation that Badiou calls the state.[5] This second structuring counts the situation as one situation. For example, a situation created from a multiplicity of entities (people, families, states, livestock, cities, villages, forests, etc.) in a certain territory and a certain historical period is counted as one situation that has the name the Kingdom of France. The second structure takes place from principle. This is because the operation of "counting-as-one" cannot count itself as one. This is why Badiou claims that the "withering away" of the state is a much more complicated process than it seemed to Lenin and other political theorists who believed that the state would wither away and be replaced with another political form. In this second structuring, the individual multiplicities counted as one are divided according to whether they are incorporated into a situation (as its subset) or they merely exist in a situation as unincorporated elements. In the first case, each element of the set is also an element of the set that illustrates the entirety of all of the given sets. In other words, these elements have the property that defines a set that is the total of all sets. As Badiou says, each element presented by the first multiplicity is also presented by the second multiplicity; that is, it is represented (doubly presented).[6] In the case that a multiplicity is an element of the given situation, but it isn't a subset within it, the elements of this multiplicity are not represented by the set that is the total of all the given multiplicities.

Returning to the previous example, the Kingdom of France is a state in which the set "aristocratic estate" is represented. The elements of this multiplicity have the property that defines the multiplicity that illustrates the entirety of the Kingdom of France (i.e., "being an aristocrat"). The prerogatives and positions within this state are accessible only to those who have this property. In principle, someone who is not an aristocrat cannot become the king, because if it were to happen, the entire structure of the Kingdom of France's state representation would fall apart. There are then other states or layers that form sets which are present in the Kingdom of France, but they are not incorporated within it as a subset; for example, there are peasants, artisans, laborers, lower clergy, and the emerging bourgeoisie. These sets are defined by properties that don't correspond to the property that defines the whole of the Kingdom of France (the property "not being an aristocrat," "being poor," "being an autonomous economic subject," etc.) These sets are elements of the set of the "Kingdom of France," but they are not represented within it.

This type of multiplicity creates an evental site. It is a multiplicity counted by the first structuring, which makes "one" multiplicity out of the multiplicity of multiplicities, and thus becomes present in the given situation ("peasants" is a unifying name for a certain multiplicity of beings who, thanks to this designation, are visible in the state of the Kingdom of France). However, this multiplicity is not counted by the second structuring, because the defining property doesn't correspond to the property that defines the whole of the Kingdom of France. Evental multiplicity is "abnormal" in the sense that it is composed of uncounted multiplicities that only exist within the situation. This multiplicity is not representable within the given state.[7] Badiou also provides the working class, the deadlock in science, and the state of artistic tendencies as examples of evental sites.[8] We could find many specific historical illustrations for this evental site. For example, in art it was a state of artistic tendencies that went beyond the academic experience of art in the second half of the nineteenth century. These tendencies manifested themselves and were counted as present, but they were not representable in the structure of experience that was reproduced by the artistic institutions of that period.[9] From the perspective of these institutions, impressionist and other tendencies seemed empty and abnormal. Due to these two properties, the evental site is on the "edge of the void" as Badiou terms it. It isn't pure emptiness, because the evental site presents itself in the given situation, but at the same time it is a multiplicity that is empty from the perspective of the state.

An evental site is a condition of an event. This fact is not appreciated by some of Badiou's critics (e.g., Daniel Bensaïd), who claim that in his theory the event has the nature of a miracle because the event allegedly occurs regardless of historical circumstances.[10] These critics assume that Badiou claims the event cannot be predicted and explained on the basis of circumstances. Its occurrence has the character of a Mallarméan roll of a die whose result is random. Badiou responded to these objections by making it more clear in his books that he never underestimated the analysis of the historical situation or capital and its tendencies. He only rejects purely academic Marxist studies that cultivate scholastic investigations into the details of Marx's theory and lack a relationship to the issue of the event or revolution in the contemporary world. Badiou organically incorporated Marxist political economy into the last book of his ontological trilogy, *The Immanence of Truths*. Here, political economy takes on a higher meaning because it's an analytical tool for revealing the economic suppression of infinity, which takes place through a closed repetition of reproductive and circulatory patterns of capital.[11]

Badiou distinguishes between the evental site and the event in order to protest against their mixing. An event may or may not occur at the evental site. There is no necessity or determination here because the evental site only creates the possibility of an event. The site is called "evental" only retroactively if the event has actually occurred.[12] Badiou defines the event as a multiplicity that is composed of elements from the evental site as well as from itself. What's crucial is that the event is an element in itself, or to put it in other words, the event belongs to itself. This self-referential relationship allows the event not to merge into its site, so that a gap appears between it and the conditions that enabled it to occur.[13] For this reason, the event cannot be deduced from historical conditions in the form of condensed social contradictions, as Althusser had written. One of the things Badiou is reacting to with his conception of the event is this theoretical shortcoming in Althusser's theory of social change. Althusser writes about the condensation of contradictions as a "revolutionary situation" that can be missed if there is no effective political intervention. Althusser's theory of society creates space for political intervention because the *effectiveness* of this intervention cannot be deduced from a particular state of contradictions or from the network of determinations (overdetermination). These are only conditions for its effectiveness, but the effectiveness itself depends on a set of various random factors, such as individual decisions made at the "right" moment, and the determination and courage to take risks that are associated with this factor, or the momentary mental and physical dispositions of those who were involved. However, Althusser lacks a term that would express this fundamentally random and self-contained structure that this political intervention introduces, which may or may not result in a revolution. However, Althusser does not define the specific features of this structure, which escapes the network of determination (overdetermination), and he doesn't thematize revolution in this way. We can understand Badiou's concept of the event and the subject as overcoming this deficit in Althusser's theory, which, however, overturns some of Althusser's conceptions.

According to Badiou, this self-referential character of the event is evoked primarily in the way that the event acquires its name, which retroactively enables a certain unification of its multiplicity. Naming an event is an act that Badiou understands as an interpretive intervention. The naming isn't given by the event itself, but must be a subsequent event that provides the event with a name and thus retroactively defines it as an event. Badiou therefore conceives of the event as an interval that lies between the empty anonymity of the multiplicity at the evental site and the assignment of a name. The event originally isn't "one," but "two." It is made up of a nameless multiplicity and its subsequent naming.[14] Badiou gives the act of naming decisive importance. If this intervention is not performed, the event isn't represented by anything, and it lacks internal coherency. Without its naming, it dissipates before it begins to act in a given situation. Certain philosophers (such as Frank Ruda) take this constitutive significance of the intervention of naming to an extreme when they understand the event itself as an effect of the naming and claim that its objectivity is a result of the line of subjective agreement on its existence.[15] However, Badiou distinguishes the event and its naming as two instances that are mutually dependent, but one does not create the other. Ruda's interpretation of the event is close to philosophical idealism. In his conception, it should be that the existence of an event is retroactively conditioned by the subjective decision to name a certain multiplicity as an event. Ruda does not take sufficient account of the fact that the objective condition of the event is a specific site that is not the result of subjective naming, but arises through a regime of representation in a given state. This objective character of the event is possible to emphasize by connecting the evental site with latencies that are an expression of immanent tendencies in the development of social contradictions. The evental site is then made up of multiplicities that incorporate elements that have been formed as social and economic tendencies. Badiou does not explicitly introduce them, but they are consistent with his theory of events.[16]

Naming an event requires a certain separation or "subtraction" from the given manner of counting multiplicities. However, the referent of this counting is emptiness, because the event still doesn't have its name, and thus from the state's perspective, it doesn't exist. But what gives rise to this subtraction from the "law" of counting? It cannot be due to the event itself, which is thus far composed of an indeterminate multiplicity without a name and which cannot be referred to as a referent. Badiou shows that there is only one possible way to subtract from the law of counting from the determined state and naming the event. This is following up on another event that has already been "decided." The referent that enables subtraction from the given law of the state is a preceding event, its name, and the effects in the form of a procedure that this event enabled. This relationship to the past event creates a subtraction from the present state. This subtraction is a condition of the interventions that name the event and thus make it into an element of the existing situation. The relationship to the past event as a reference point is a necessary condition for the naming of the present event, without which this event dissipates and its place remains empty. In this way, Badiou explains why at the beginning of every political revolution there is a return to the past and a reference to previous revolutions, and their movements and figures: The French Revolution thus referred to the Roman Republic, the Paris Commune referred to the French Revolution, and the October Revolution used the Paris Commune as its reference point. Badiou mentions the Shanghai Commune from the period of the Chinese Cultural Revolution as the last established political form that belongs to the sequence of the communist idea in the twentieth century. As stated above, the Shanghai Commune was an experiment in "politics without a party." It was to overcome the unresolved contradiction of this sequence, which was the connection of the revolutionary process with the institution of the state, which suffocated this process even though at the beginning it had been seen as a necessary means to defend the revolution. It's remarkable that the Shanghai Commune chose the Paris Commune as its reference point, which was what the founding event of the entire sequence—the October Revolution—was related to.

There exists a notion that the event doesn't require a reference point in the past, that it is a radical beginning and that the intervention of naming is legitimized on its own basis. Thus, the idea that it is possible to refuse any kind of connection to past events and create an absolutely new type of event is put forth. Badiou calls this speculative leftism. Speculative leftism is unaware that the event exists only to the extent that it's connected with a given regime of counting. The fascination with the world Revolution without a relationship to past events always leads to a Manichean hypostasis of the event. Naming the event in this "pure" form separates the event from ambiguous consequences, failure, and its degradation in the past, but it also makes it impossible for the event that is understood in this speculative manner to develop into the long-term lines of action that require discipline.[17] Badiou demonstrates that the very naming of an event requires a certain relationship to a past event that has been historically closed. If this relationship did not exist, we couldn't name the event in such a way that it is retroactively established and begins to circulate in a given regime of counting. A new event requires a name that is sufficiently intelligible; that is, it is counted in the given situation, and thanks to this it acquires a certain definition that allows people to join it. If there were an absolutely new name, the event would remain outside of known connections and would be inaccessible. At the same time, there is no direct link to the past event, because its truth procedures have already closed. There appears a mystery of the relationship to historically closed truth-events, which I have written about above in connection with Badiou's situation in the interregnum. As we will see, this mystery appears in the very core of Badiou's philosophy.

Badiou designates the name of the event as "ultra-one." This expresses the basic feature of the event, which is the fact that it is a multiplicity that isn't incorporated into the given situation and only exists within it as one. It is a paradoxical multiplicity that is empty from the perspective of the state. The name of the event is therefore a naming and a presentation of that which appears like emptiness in the state: as a multiplicity that doesn't exist. The name of the event is a signifier that has the form of a signified, which expresses nothing in the given situation and which lacks a place in the structure of meanings determined by the established manner of representation. For this reason, Badiou claims that the name of the event is superfluous. It's a name that counts as one something that doesn't exist. According to Badiou's definition, the event is a multiplicity that is an element of itself. The name of the event is an element of the event because it is the result of the intervention of naming. Through this intervention, the multiplicity is counted as one, which does not belong to the counting done in the regime of the state. It is one that doesn't rely on any pregiven regime of counting. It is one that presents itself because it stands outside the regime of counting (it's superfluous). Badiou introduces the expression ultra-one for the name of the event because it expresses a self-referential form of counting.[18]

Badiou always examines the event from two perspectives. The first is the present situation, which is structured by the given state. The second is the event itself and its consequences. The name of the event has to be known in the given situation, and it is thus counted as one.[19] From the perspective of the situation, the name of the event is indistinguishable from other names whose meaning is determined by counting in the state. For example, the name Spartacus is known in this way and is counted. However, it is also a name that can be used to name an event and retroactively establish it. For example, the event led by Rosa Luxemburg and Karl Liebknecht in Germany in 1919 was named the Spartacist uprising.[20] Participants in the uprising refer to a name from the past that enables them to separate from the given state, in which the name of Spartacus is counted in such a way that his rebellious significance belongs only in the past. However, the name Spartacus gives a name to and unifies a multiplicity of political activities, protests, and slogans that appeared in Germany in 1919. From the perspective of the given state (Gustav Noske's government), this plurality is a mere disruption of order that is necessary to suppress and normalize. However, the unifying name of Spartacus gives meaning to this multiplicity that isn't acceptable to the state. This meaning is an event whose existence is undecidable. The name Spartacus, as a label for an event, is superfluous from the perspective of the state, and from the perspective of the event, it represents an ultra-one.

Truth as a Generic Procedure

The second fundamental concept of Badiou's philosophy is truth as a generic procedure, in which we also find a specific relationship between multiplicity and unity. The generic procedure is essentially identical to the concept of the truth procedure, and the truth procedure is its operator. The generic procedure creates consequences of the event, which enter into the given situation and transform it. An event that lacks consequences would remain a merely speculative possibility that emerges at a certain place and is then extinguished at the same place without leaving a trace. It would be a flare-up of a possibility with nothing following, so we can only speculate whether the event did occur and what consequences it would have had if it had developed a generic procedure. An event with a generic procedure is an event with truth, and therefore it's a formation that falls apart into the multiplicity of multiplicities that dissolves into the situation determined by the state. The basis of a generic procedure is the fidelity of the event, thanks to which the consequences of the event can emerge. Badiou doesn't understand fidelity only as a moral quality. It is mainly an operation that is always performed at a particular site, and it has a functional relationship to the event. It consists in searching for the multiplicities that can be attached to the event. The count-as-one takes place within the framework of this operation. However, multiplicities are counted in a manner that escapes the counting within a given state. This operation performs a subtraction from the state and then a counting procedure in which the multiplicities are presented in their specific place as multiplicities that belong to the state and the counting in which these multiplicities are presented in their specific place as multiplicities that belong to the event. When performing the event counting, fidelity rearranges the multiplicities of the situation and creates a new structure for them, which can appear to be against the state.[21] The faithful operation combines unity and multiplicity within itself. It is an operation that is unified and universal in its function because, at various places, it connects multiplicities to a single event, and its connection takes the form of counting the event as one. However, generic fidelity to an event does not create a universal criterion according to which it's possible to determine which connections are correct and which are not. In another context, Badiou calls the fidelity that is focused on creating this kind of generally valid criterion "dogmatic fidelity."[22] It is possible to distinguish what belongs to an event in every situation on the basis of multiple criteria, and even multiple faithful procedures, at the same time, and often there is disunity and strife between them. Badiou cites the Stalinists and

Trotskyists as an example: both groups proclaimed their fidelity to the events of October 1917, but at the same time they also massacred each other. Both the institutions and mathematicians who developed set theory claimed to be faithful to the evental crisis that was caused at the beginning of the twentieth century by logical paradoxes within logic and mathematics. However, they then developed logic and mathematics in an entirely different way. Similarly, serialist composers and later also neoclassicist composers derived the reverse consequences from the chromatic distribution of the tonal system.[23] Badiou creates a general theory of fidelity in which it is a priori impossible to determine which direction of the inference of consequences is faithful to the event. According to Badiou, in principle, there is a multiplicity of faithful procedures that relate to one event.

However, the qualitative aspects of the fidelity procedure can serve as an orientation point in determining individual directions that make claims to apply to the same event. Badiou provides a total of three: the first side of fidelity is its deductive character, which contains a certain dogmatism. Fidelity examines the multiplicity and the propositions in conformity with whether they can be deduced from previous propositions that arose during the event's unfolding. If the proposition is in contradiction with these event propositions, fidelity refuses to connect them to the event. Fidelity ensures the coherence of the entire procedure. The second qualitative aspect of fidelity is its spontaneous nature. It is spontaneous because it searches for multiplicities and propositions that are not a mechanical reproduction of already-attached multiplicities and propositions, but which have meanings that are unpredictable. These spontaneously discovered multiples are attached to the event on the basis of their formal coherence with the current faithful procedure. However, their content is not a repetition of the previous elements of the faithful procedure, and therefore these connected spontaneous instances create unknown directions for the event's development. The third qualitative side of fidelity lies in its genericness. This term refers to Cohen's discovery of generic sets; however, in this context, it expresses the creative power of fidelity, which invents undescribed relationships between the elements of the situation, reworks existing relationships, and dares to make seemingly absurd connections. This faithful activity has an experimental character: through its experimental steps, fidelity creates polymorphic formations that are situated at the intersection of various directions of the event's development.[24]

Based on this qualitative criterion, we can understand the extinction of truth procedures as an extinction of spontaneity and genericness. These two qualities created new ways of developing an event, and the truth procedure was enlivened with the principle of the unexpected. Their extinction is a symptom of the truth procedure becoming connected with the structures of a state, which has no place for spontaneity and genericness. This connection closes the truth procedure, and an era arrives in which the truth ceases to operate: that is, an interregnum. The question lingers of whether it's possible for a state to exist that has structures in which spontaneity and the genericness of truth procedures are able to develop. Badiou leaves this question open.

The Subject as a Temporal Operator

In Badiou's philosophy, the generic procedure is closely connected with the subject, which is also a relationship of unity and multiplicity, and this is a type that we cannot classify as postmodern or modern thinking. In Badiou's view, the subject isn't a phenomenological knowledge that organizes human experience, nor is it Cartesian substance, nor does it correspond to the Lacanian void or the poststructuralist effect of discursive practices. The subject is a local configuration of the generic procedure.[25] Badiou distinguishes individual subjects (love), mixed subjects; that is, the connection of individuals with a particular community (science, art), and collective subjects (politics). Individuals, communities, groups, and organizations are not made into subjects by their mere existence, but they become subjects, as Badiou says, in rare cases.[26] As we have seen, the generic procedure consists in discovering and connecting certain elements of a situation to an event (to its name). However, there isn't a clear guideline that would determine which elements to connect and which not to. The subject is an instance that performs both the operation of connecting and the operation of not connecting without having an objectively granted assurance that it is proceeding correctly. It cannot rely on the event itself or on the consequences that have developed so far, because it encounters multiplicities whose connection or non-connection has not yet been decided upon. Neither the event nor its consequences determine the further course of the generic procedure. The subject cannot arise either out of the available knowledge (data, information, statistics, surveys), which is structured according to the regime of the state.[27] Badiou terms the knowledge that forces this multiplicity into pre-prepared categories the encyclopedia. From this perspective of this knowledge, it isn't possible to distinguish whether elements belong to the event, because the encyclopedia doesn't have any category adequate for the event itself, and therefore, there is none for it. The subject isn't the result of determination either from the side of the event or the side of the situation.

There are two levels that appear in this *indetermination* of the subject. The first level is the origin of the subject. The individual or community intervenes in the given situation and connects certain multiplicities from it to the event. According to Badiou, it isn't possible to decide from the perspective of the situation whether the event exists as an element of it, and therefore the individual or community is in a position that corresponds to the "axiom of choice." He says that for every multiplicity of multiplicities, there exists a multiplicity composed of selected elements of non-empty multiplicities that represent this multiplicity. We can understand the selection of elements as meaning that for every multiplicity there is a function that "chooses" the elements that are its representations.[28] Interventions into the given situation mean that we "choose" elements out of the given multiplicities that make up this multiplicity that contains their representation. In other words, the axiom of choice makes it possible to claim that an event exists as a multiplicity whose elements are selected from the multiplicities that belong to the situation. The function of choice, which expresses the nature of the intervention, establishes the subject. The individual or community is a multiplicity that belongs to the situation. Whether it makes a "choice" and transfers certain elements from the multiplicities that it encounters into the multiplicity that has been given the name of an event, this is an act that causes it to emerge as a subject. This act is not determined by the event itself, nor is it determined even by knowledge that corresponds to the state's regime. There is then a second level, which concerns subsequent operations that are performed in connecting or not connecting certain multiplicities to the event. These operations also have the character of the axiom of choice, and we can understand them as a repetition of the intervention that brought the subject into existence. At this level, the subject is made up of configurations of results of its selection of evental and non-evental elements of the situation. Deducibility offers a certain guideline for making choices among multiplicities out of the evental multiplicities (the dogmatic element), but it is an insufficient guideline because the truth procedure has to also contain a non-deducible element of spontaneity and genericness.

Simply put, an individual or community becomes a subject if it makes Pascal's wager on the existence of an event that can be called an axiomatic choice in the sense that it's a claim about the existence of something that cannot be proved.[29] This wager is always connected with the risk that the event doesn't exist, that it is a mere chimera. The only indicator of its existence is the potentiality of its development, which, however, we only recognize on the basis of its consequences in a given situation. This potentiality doesn't have the nature of a seed that grows into a tree of consequences, but it is a potentiality that arises retroactively on the basis of generic procedures that, on the basis of choice, have assigned certain multiplicities to the event. These multiplicities were not part of the event in the form of its internal potentiality in the Aristotelian sense. Their emergence and their connection to the event are not predetermined by the event itself, because this is the work of the subject.

The existence of an event in a given situation cannot become the object of knowledge. But what form does the relationship between the subject and the event have if the subject doesn't recognize the event as a certain fact or a provable proposition? Badiou chooses the concept of faith for this form of relationship. On the basis of its Pascal wager, the subject believes that a truth exists. In its recognition of the multiplicities that belong to the event, the subject cannot satisfactorily prove that this activity relates to something verifiable in the terms of knowledge referred to as an encyclopedia. Badiou conceives of faith in two ways. On the one hand, it's a faith in the existence of an event, and on the other, it's faith as belief in a future in which the situation that has been structured according to the event and its generic procedures ("an emancipated society") arises.[30] This new situation retroactively interprets the previous situation so that the event and its consequences existed within it. It is only with this retroactive process that the event becomes the object of knowledge. The arrival of a new situation cannot be conceived deterministically as a necessary result of a certain movement of generic procedures. Badiou does not admit any teleology of history, because the approach of generic procedures is dependent on the operations of subjects that are indeterministic.

Badiou does not understand the subject in a Manichean way: the subject undertakes operations that relate to the event and believes in the arrival of a new situation, but these operations are not entirely separated from the knowledge that exists as the encyclopedia of the given state. Badiou formulates the "fundamental law of the subject" as a law of the future perfect tense. According to this law, forcing takes place between the statements of the subject's language that relates to the event and the statements of the given situation. Forcing is an approach created by Paul Cohen for set theory, and Badiou uses it in his philosophy as a method for coherently thinking about the relationship between a set that is made up of evental multiplicities and a set that is made of elements that belong to the situation. These two sets contain elements for which it is impossible to determine to which set they belong. Badiou expresses philosophical forcing in such a way that if a statement of the subject's language becomes verified (*véridique*) after the situation arises in which the truth appears (a future state), it's because there exists some element in the present situation that belongs to this truth (to the generic procedure i.e. the truth) and at the same time it also maintains its relationship to the statements that are part of the encyclopedic knowledge of the given state.[31]

Badiou provides a simple example from Newtonian astronomy. We observe a deviation in a planet's orbit and make calculations that show the deviation is caused by a factor that cannot yet be identified. We call it a planet. The operator of the connection of the statement about the existence of other planets is the calculation on the basis of previously made observation. The statement "another planet exists" will be verified only when the model of the solar system is established and supplemented with this planet. We can say that until then, such a statement doesn't make sense because it isn't verifiable. We lack knowledge about the "relationship between 'something is inflecting the trajectory' (a statement composed of names of science—and 'something' indicates that one of these names is empty) and *a* term of the situation, a specifiable term (a planet with a calculable mass) whose scientifically observable existence in the solar system (that is, this system, plus its truth) would give meaning and veracity to my statement."[32] The existence of "something" that is inflecting the planet's trajectory is not verifiable in the given encyclopedia of knowledge because this existence doesn't correspond to the term "the planet" as an object that is observable and occupies a certain place in the solar system. However, its existence is verifiable if we are going to have the possibility to observe this "something." The claim originally wasn't verifiable, but it became so.[33] This example illustrates that forcing as a fundamental law of the subject leads to the subject of the generic procedure being created out of statements that aren't verifiable in a given situation, but they are statements that can be verifiable in a future situation. Thus, statements that are in principle unverifiable have no possible referent, such as the terms "good" or "revolution" in their purely abstract meanings (which we encounter in speculative leftism) do not belong to the truth procedure.

The subject is a formation that contains three temporal levels. In the form of faith, it relates to the event and its name. The event took place in the past, but its effects linger in the present through the subject, which connects elements of the given situation to the name of the event in the generic procedure. The verb tense that expresses the event in relation to the subject is the present perfect, which captures the lingering consequences of the past action in the present. The subject moves in the present in its search for multiplicities that can be connected to the name of the event. Its second verb tense is the present continuous, and its third is the future perfect, which expresses the faith of the subject that a situation will come in which the truth-event will appear and it will structure this situation. This makes the elements of the truth procedure verifiable. In connection with the subject, Badiou writes only about the future perfect, but there isn't any reason not to express the subject's time span through the present perfect and the present continuous as well.

Subject is the final arrangement of the generic procedure and it represents only a fragment of it that is found at a specific point in time at a specific place. The truth, however, is a hypothetical whole composed of the results of all the faithful operations relating to the given event, and therefore it's infinite. The subject, as a finite formation, is incommensurable with the infinitude of the truth. In Badiou's conception, the subject lacks unmediated access to the truth because it doesn't know the truth.[34] The subject is a temporal and local fragment of the truth as a potentially infinite generic procedure, and the truth is transcendent in relation to it. The subject is defined by its fidelity to the event, but the meaning of this event isn't fixed to a certain temporal and local configuration of the generic procedure. For example, the significance of the event in modern music is not only limited to the atonal music developed by Schönberg and his successors, and the significance of the October Revolution is not exhausted by the meaning of the "workers' party."

The Retrocausality of the Unity and the Multiplicity

In this study of Badiou's categories of the event, truth, and the subject, we have encountered forms of multiplicity and unity that are not merely variations of their patterns that we find in postmodernism, modernism, or earlier philosophical movements. This novelty of Badiou's philosophy arises from the fact that his manner of thinking isn't formed by the structures of language, as was the case—other than a few exceptions—in the history of philosophy, because Badiou's thinking is "conditioned" by the mathematical discoveries of the multiplicity of multiplicities, the generic set, forcing, etc., which were previously unavailable to philosophy. Multiplicity and unity are patterns that arise as a result of the operation of counting the multiplicity of multiplicities, and thus they are not concepts that could serve as a basis for ontological thinking. We can understand Badiou's categories of the event, truth, and the subject as a composition of relationships between multiplicity and unity in which, however, at the basic interpretive level, these patterns take the form of a multiplicity of multiplicities and of the operator of the count-as-one procedure. The category of the event is a combination of multiplicity and unity in which both take several forms. The event is connected with the evental site, which is a multiplicity counted as one, whose elements, however, are not counted as one in the regime of the state's representation. The event is also connected with the ultra-one, which is its name that enables the counting of its elements that are not counted by the state. Badiou conceives the event as a multiplicity that acquires its unity through the ultra-one. It is a type of unification that takes place through retroactive intervention in which the multiplicity of the event is named. In Badiou's conception, the event is constituted through a double operation. It arises because, on the one hand, there is an event as a multiplicity (a multiplicity of the evental site and the relationship of finding this multiplicity to itself) and an event as a retroactive intervention that connects a name with the function of ultra-one to this event. The unity is an instance that arises after a certain time has elapsed following the multiplicity of the event, but it has a constitutive meaning for the event. There is a temporal gap that lies between the first instance (the evental multiplicity) and the second instance (the unifying ultra-one). However, this second instance adds as a condition of the first instance. Although the event as a multiplicity precedes the event as a unity, it only begins to exist in the mode of counting when the second instance occurs. An event would not exist as a multiplicity if the intervention of naming hadn't taken place. This is because Badiou conceives of the multiplicity with regard to the situation as inconsistent and its contents as empty or invisible. This is what the content is during the time when it still hasn't been counted with the name that has the function of ultra-one. If, in a situation, there exists only that which is presented as one and the event is not counted as one through the intervention, the event is not an element of the situation and therefore doesn't exist. Although the existence of the event is unverifiable and invisible from the perspective of the situation, its multiplicity must be counted as one so that the faithful procedure can come into existence. If the event were to remain merely multiple, there isn't anything to be faithful to. This event doesn't exist either from the perspective of individuals or communities who would be the ones whose behavior creates the event as a pure multiplicity.

Multiplicity and unity are not two separate poles, but there is a relationship between them that can be expressed like a loop in time or retrocausality (retractive causality). Badiou does not introduce this notion when describing an event, but it seems to me like a theoretical model that will help us better understand the retroactivity acting in events. Retrocausality is a term used in quantum physics, where it describes a paradoxical relationship between cause and effect: the effect precedes its cause in time, or a later event acts upon a previous event. In the set of elements that have the property of "being a cause," it's a subset of elements that have the property of "being the effect of causes." Retrocausality contradicts our intuition and acts as a paradox, but as the Nobel Prize winner in physics (1965) Richard P. Feynman proved, there are entirely coherent equations that express the phenomenon of retrocausality (e.g., an electron, which acts as a cause in itself).[35] Retrocausality is a term formulated in quantum physics, from which it follows that the effect of a time-sequential event on an event preceding it is intellectually coherent. Badiou's concept of the event that contains this retrocausality can thus also be considered coherent. Here, we encounter the retroactive effect of unity in the form of the name of the event (ultra-one) on our own conditions, which is the event as a multiplicity. In this action, the effect of unity is its own cause, because the unity as the name of the event arises when there is an event. However, this is the effect of its naming. In time, the naming of an event follows after the event has occurred, but the naming retroactively creates its own assumption, which is this event. We can express their mutual conditionality with a certain simplification so that unity is a condition of the existence of multiplicity, and multiplicity is a condition for the existence of unity.

The second fundamental category of Badiou's philosophy, which is the truth of the generic procedure, shows a similar relationship between plurality and unity. The generic procedure is a term for the consequences of the event that are inscribed into a given situation. As has been said, in principle, one event can have many concurrent generic procedures. There is not a sufficiently general criterion that would determine which generic procedure is more faithful to the event, even though there are ancillary criteria (deductibility, spontaneity, genericity). The generic procedure is unified by its entire sequence relating to one event (the name of the event). If several generic procedures are developed concurrently, they have a common unifying moment in the name of the event, even if there is strife and enmity between them. An example is the symbolism of the color red, which marks a common founding event for the diverse and often quarreling emancipatory currents in the twentieth century. The generic procedure is both random and multiple because it develops by connecting multiplicities that it encounters in various places in the given situation to the event. The generic procedure defines the pluralities defined by the state (e.g., social classes or works of art) according to a different principle than the one given by the regime of counting. This principle is belonging or not belonging to the event. The generic procedure introduces the figure of two into the situation and brings in a diagonal line that crosses the lines determined by the given state. The field of multiplicities (social classes, works of art, etc.) is rearranged according to whether or not they can be connected to the event. The attached multiplicities are defined by a common property, which is "belong to the name of the event," which means that they are newly defined by this name, which acts as a counting ultra-one. The attached multiplicities are still counted by the given situation, and therefore they retain their differences. They do not give rise to a multiplicity of mutually equivalent elements. On the one hand, the generic procedure creates a unification of these multiplicities on the basis of their connection to one event; however, these multiplicities are mutually distinct because they are different elements of the given situation. They take on the property of "belonging to the (name) event," which unifies them and at the same time a difference is created with the other multiplicities which lack this property in the given situation. The unity creates a difference with the symbolized figure of "two" (the property "belonging to the event" and the property of "not belonging to the event"). This difference conditions the further development of unity in the sense of the sequence of operations related to the single event (the name of the event). In another form, there is the mutual conditionality of unity and multiplicity that we already encountered when examining the event.

The third fundamental category of Badiou's philosophy is the subject. As stated before, the subject is always a multiplicity that exists in one place inside the situation, and this multiplicity is the operator of connecting and not connecting multiplicities to the event. However, if the subject were only a multiplicity, the operation of connecting/not connecting wouldn't be possible. What would the subject connect or not connect if it, itself, were defined merely by its place within the situation? Such a subject would be indistinguishable from the multiplicity defined by the given situation. If we did not connect the subject with a form of unity that exceeds its place in the given situation, it would not be a subject, but an individual, a community, or an organization that at a certain place repeats the counting operation in conformity with the state regime. The rejection of the principle of unity and the absolutization of the multiplicity necessarily leads to conformism to the given situation. The unity lies in the fact that the subject as a finite multiplicity within space and time believes in the existence of the event as an element of the given situation, even though this event isn't verifiable within the situation. The form of the unity of the subject is belief in the event and its consequences, which are the truth procedures. The subject relates to the event through the truth, which represents a line of the event's consequences that retroactively appear like a unified line. In this sense, the subject is an operator of the unification of the existing truth procedure because it needs a guideline for distinguishing evental pluralities from non-evental pluralities in the given situation. The unification of the event's existing consequences is a prerequisite for its further development. Badiou speaks about their deducibility from the existing generic procedure. If the new multiplicity is to be deducible from the previous consequences of the event, these consequences must have some unified form. This is why retroactive unifying generic procedures take place: for example, in church history, the multiplicity of influences, layers of text, and intellectual sources are retroactively conceived as a unified canon, such as the New Testament or Orthodox doctrine. Unity is a condition for the continuation of the generic procedure and the subject, which has connected previously unknown multiplicities to the event. The unification of the generic procedure fulfills the requirement of deducibility that Badiou terms the dogmatic element. The unification of this procedure enables the subject to proceed spontaneously and generically when performing its operation. Dogmatism in this sense acts as a condition of spontaneity and creativity.

The subject is also defined by the axiom of choice. The connection/non-connection of a certain multiplicity to the event is an intervention that isn't determined either by the presently existing truth procedure or by the situation in the state regime. Its connection/non-connection becomes part of the generic procedure when the subject isn't led by deducibility, but also by spontaneity and genericity. The subject's intervention always means an interruption of the unified procedure and the establishment of a certain disunity. If the principle of the choice of the multiplicity were a continuation of unity, only the principle of deducibility would apply, so the procedure would cease to be generic and therefore a truth procedure. At the moment of intervention, the unifying activity is suspended and the perspective of the plurality dominates. If the unifying activity is to continue as a retroactive forming of the generic procedure, it's necessary for the subject to focus on the uniqueness of the given plurality and to discover qualities in it that would remain invisible when applying the requirement of unity. The subject discovers these qualities spontaneously and generically. They are qualities thanks to which the procedure continues as a generic and truth procedure and not only as a repetitive procedure.

The subject is a formation that retroactively creates the unity of the generic procedure, and as a local configuration of the generic procedure, this is the way it becomes a multiplicity with a unified form. However, this form is temporarily suspended as soon as the intervention is performed, and the subject connects a multiplicity to the event on the basis of its spontaneous and generic search for its uniqueness. There is a similar retrocausality here, as there had been in Badiou's previous categories. The unity of the generic procedure created by the subject is an effect whose cause is the existence of multiplicities that are connected to one event (truth). The connections are conditioned by the unity of the generic procedure. Unity is an effect which, in this sense, is the cause of itself because it is caused by what this effect itself enabled (the connection of multiplicities to a single event). The subject is an arrangement of a generic procedure (truth) in a certain place at a certain time, in which the multiplicity in the form of generic connections of multiplicities to the event is conditioned by the unity of the presently existing generic procedure. This unity is conditioned by these operations of multiplicity.

Badiou's Philosophy as a Ladder over the Interregnum

My hypothesis was that the event, truth, and subject, which are the fundamental categories in Badiou's philosophy, express a new type of unity and plurality that does not show the circulation between unity and plurality that distinguishes formations of the interregnum. Closer examination has demonstrated that these categories express a relationship between unity and plurality that I have termed retrocausal. Unity and plurality are mutually conditioned here in the form of the retroaction of one instance upon the other. The unity of an event is the result of a naming intervention that acts upon the event as a multiplicity and makes it its own causal condition. Truth as a generic procedure is a multiplicity of individual multiplicities connected to the event, and its procedure is conditioned by its retroactive unification. The subject is a multiplicity of faithful operations that are accomplished by connecting the multiplicities of a situation to the event. The subject has the form of the axiom of choice, which is, however, conditioned by a retroactive unification of the multiplicity of its operations. No circulations are taking place here in which unity and multiplicity are two poles that give rise to the idea of predetermined concepts. In the metamodernist description of contemporary cultural formations, there should be an oscillation between the desire for an event and a truth, and the negation of this desire, which is caused by getting too close to the pole of the event and truth. Similarly, in an elliptical model, the development of the event would cause a circulation movement to the second focal point, which is the state. In its vicinity, conformist reproduction of the "encyclopedia" determined by the state would take place, and this would negate the results of the development of the event. This negation would lead to a temporary affirmation of the regime of the state. Here, the subject would represent the operator of this circulation between the truth-event and the state, and it would be a truly schizophrenic subject. However, we have seen that Badiou defines the subject by its interventions in the field of multiplicities of the situation and by its axiomatic relationship to (the name of) the event. Elliptical circulations or metamodernist oscillations take place in those individuals or communities that have not become a subject. The circulations and oscillations of formations that belong to the interregnum are, from the point of view of Badiou's philosophy, a sign of the pre-subject form of existence. Badiou conceives of the subject as the operator of fidelity to the event, which is conditioned by the affirmation of the truth. As soon as a circulation of this type, which characterizes the forms of the interregnum, occurs, the subject begins to turn into an individual or a community that is incorporated into a non-evental situation.

Returning to the original hypotheses formulated as Thesis A and Thesis B (in the subchapter "Do truths exist in the interregnum? Mysteries of Badiou's philosophy"), we can state that

THESIS A: Badiou's philosophy belongs among the formations of the interregnum that show circulations between unity and plurality, between truth and the impossibility of its full presence, and so on, INVALID.

THESIS B: Badiou's philosophy has created a new beginning of a "doctrine of truths," but it doesn't show a circulation typical for formations in the interregnum. Badiou's philosophy represents a formation that, because of its structure, does not arise from the interregnum and only belongs to it because it arose in the conditions of the interregnum, VALID.

Badiou created a conception of the subject that isn't incorporated into the situation of the interregnum because it's a formation in which the affirmation of truth and the event create the condition of its existence. The event and truth are formations created in such a way that allow their affirmation to take place even in the situation of the interregnum. The event and the truth are a composition of multiplicity and unity in which there are two instances in a retrocausal relationship. The multiplicity and the truth are not opposites, because the multiplicity is conditioned by unity and the unity is conditioned by multiplicity. By contrast with interregnum formations, an elliptical circulation or metamodernist oscillation does not arise in them. The subject who affirms the event and truth finds unity in as well as multiplicity in it where the unity doesn't stimulate a repulsive reaction that creates a desire for the disruption of the unity. Nor does a repulsive reaction arise in the case of the multiplicity. This reaction was the motive force of elliptical circulations and metamodernist oscillations. If unity and plurality have a mutually conditioned relationship and they do not create these reactions, there is no motive force that would create these circulations or oscillations. For this reason, I claim that event, truth, and the subject are not connected with either a circulation movement or with oscillations. Thus, Thesis B is confirmed as valid: Badiou's philosophy differs from the formations of the interregnum. This is demonstrated in the internal structures of their fundamental categories. And these are categories that indicate the possibility of an exodus from the interregnum.

Badiou created his fundamental categories in the conditions of the interregnum; that is, after the closing of truths. Their origin is not conditioned by the presently operating truth procedures (with the exception of mathematics). Now we know that Thesis B is valid, but there remain some mysteries that were mentioned above: the question of how philosophy is even possible in this situation and what the loyal subject is relating to after the closing of the truth procedures.

We cannot know how Badiou's philosophy would have changed if there were not only truths in the domain of science (mathematics) but also in the domain of politics, art, and love. In other words, we are unable to determine how Badiou's philosophy would have developed if we were outside the situation of the interregnum and all four kinds of truths were *currently* conditioning philosophy. Badiou's philosophy looks like Schopenhauer's or Wittgenstein's ladder. Schopenhauer used the metaphor of a ladder when he wrote about knowledge. "But to him who studies in order to gain insight books and studies are only steps of the ladder by which he climbs to the summit of knowledge. As soon as a round of the ladder has raised him a step, he leaves it behind him. The many, on the other hand, who study in order to fill their memory do not use the rounds of the ladder to mount by, but take them off, and load themselves with them to carry them away, rejoicing at the increasing weight of the burden. They remain always below, because they bear what ought to have borne them."[36] Following Schopenhauer, Wittgenstein used the metaphor of a ladder at the end of his *Tractatus*. While Schopenhauer leaves his ladder standing, Wittgenstein throws his ladder away: ". . . he who understands me finally recognizes them as senseless, when he has climbed out through them, on them, over them. (He must so to speak throw away the ladder, after he has climbed up on it.) He must surmount these propositions; then he sees the world rightly."[37] Badiou does not use this metaphor, but it can be aptly applied to capture his philosophy, which is built on the soil of the interregnum, but we are able to climb out of the interregnum on it. Badiou's philosophy represents a ladder that must be climbed so that we can catch a glimpse of the outlines of the world after the end of the interregnum and so that we will one day be able to leave this ladder behind us, even if in the present situation we don't know whether this isn't ultimately the only thing that will be left for us. Badiou's philosophy is a ladder made of the material that was available to him in the given historical situation. The rungs of the ladder are made from the solid material of mathematical truths that enable climbing, but some of them are broken or missing entirely. These are the rungs that represent the presently absent political and artistic truths, and the truth of love. If Badiou had not discovered the material of the "doctrine of truth" in mathematical theory, the ladder would not have its solid rungs and it would be impossible to ascend on it. If all the rungs were complete and solid, it would mean that we could easily use it to climb one floor higher and we would cease to understand it as a value in itself. In the interregnum situation, Badiou's ladder acts as an ascent to a higher floor that has not yet been built. Thanks to him, however, we can see the situation of the interregnum from above, recognize its overall condition, and the places in which the situation is beginning to shift. In the interregnum, Badiou's ladder has value in itself, but after the beginning of the new period of political and artistic truths, and truths of love, it will become a link between the situation of the interregnum and a new period of truths. At that time, his philosophy will be understood as a *transitive ontology* that creates the ontological foundations for a transition to a new period of truths. It will be possible to throw away this ladder when the new period is established as a unique world. Until then, Badiou's ladder, supplemented with new rungs, will serve as a support for building the higher floor. As stated above, Schopenhauer leaves the ladder of knowledge standing, and Wittgenstein throws it away. Badiou's philosophy will be left in place at the beginning of the new period of truths similarly to Schopenhauer's treatment of his ladder. Only later, in a hypothetical situation full of developed truths and their philosophies that is difficult to imagine today, will it be possible to cease using Badiou's philosophy as a ladder that connects the interregnum and the new period of truths. However, we will not throw the ladder of Badiou's *transitive ontology* away, but we'll preserve it as a valuable testimony to the period of transition between the interregnum and the new period of truths.

3

The Interregnum as the Age of the Absolute

The Key to Decoding the Mysteries of Badiou's Philosophy

In our investigation so far, we have repeatedly touched upon the problem of how to interpret the relationship between Badiou's philosophy and closed truth procedures when we know that Badiou believes that all four types of truths are necessary to condition the existence of philosophy. This problem wasn't solved even with Badiou's penchant for mathematics and the creation of a new "doctrine of truth." Philosophy finds itself in a situation where it isn't conditioned by the previous truths, and the new ones still haven't arrived. In the strict sense, therefore, it should not exist in the interregnum.

The second problem is closely related to this. If truths have closed in the interregnum and the subject is defined by fidelity to truth-events, what is the subject faithful to if we leave aside the specific case of mathematical truths? How can we imagine fidelity in a situation when truths currently don't exist and we can only find their scattered fragments with unclear meanings? Is the interregnum a time when fidelity is structurally impossible and the conditions for the origin of the subject are absent? Or will we find in Badiou's philosophy something other than the truth-event, something that the subject is loyal to? We can add one more mystery to these, which is related to the metaphor of the ladder over the interregnum. Badiou's philosophy is created from the categories of truth, the event, and the subject, which show that it is possible to exit the interregnum. But what leads a philosopher to even begin to build a ladder that he will erect on the soil of the interregnum if there aren't any truths that would condition this kind of activity?

I believe that the key to decoding these mysteries is offered in Badiou's distinction of truth and ideas. In *The Communist Hypothesis*, he writes that the subject of the idea gradually began appearing in his work in the late 1980s, beginning with *Manifesto for Philosophy*, where he understands his philosophy as a "Platonism of multiplicity." In *Logics of Worlds*, he approaches the concept of the idea as an ethical imperative. "Real life" is the one we live in conformity with the Idea, thus acting contrary to the principle of contemporary democratic materialism, which charges us with living without an Idea.[1] In the *Second Manifesto for Philosophy*, Badiou examined the subject of the Idea in more detail; however, he mainly focused on the process of "ideation," by which the "animal human being" becomes the subject of truth. Thanks to the idea, the individual (or collective) sees an activity that belongs to the truth procedure in his or her thoughts and actions. The Idea evokes in the subject a universalizing transformation of his or her relationship to truth. The subject realizes that it has the desire for everyone to be able to participate in the truth. It lives with the fact that its share of the truth doesn't give it the right to a particular appropriation in the truth.[2] In this way, Badiou distinguishes the truth as a procedure that is performed at a certain place in a certain time, and the idea, which gives this truth its universality and eternity.

The difference between truth and the idea stands out even more clearly in Badiou's books *The Communist Hypothesis* and *The Meaning of Sarkozy*, in which he writes about truth-events that had their specific historical incarnations in the Paris Commune and the October Revolution. These incarnations represented individual sequences of the communist idea. Truth-events and the communist idea are related to each other in a certain way, but at the same time, there is also a difference between them, because the closing of the communist sequences connected with the specific historical situation doesn't mean the end of the communist idea. Badiou does not have a Platonic understanding of the idea as one that is eternal and independent of our world, but at the same time, he refuses to subordinate it to the order of time and deconstruct it as a temporary configuration of certain textual or social effects. In these books, Badiou creates various versions of the relationship between the idea and a multiplicity-conditioned material of truths and situations (the idea as an imperative, the idea as ideation, the idea as a universalization and perpetuation of truths), but it is only in *The Immanence of Truths* that he presents a comprehensive, integrated, and complex theory of ideas that he conceives of as a form of the absolute.[3] Badiou proceeds on the basis of mathematical types of infinity, connected with the large cardinals that, in the hierarchy of infinities (countable and uncountable), represent the greatest infinities that can be formulated in mathematics. In this book, I found the key to decoding the mysteries of Badiou's philosophy.

The Absolute inside the World

In *The Immanence of Truths*, Badiou developed the terms that were already present in embryonic form in his previous books. In the *Second Manifesto for Philosophy*, the idea was primarily understood in relation to the subject as a process of ideation. In *The Immanence of Truths*, the idea moves from the sphere of the subject to the opposite pole in meaning, which is, so to speak, its objective existence, which Badiou connects with the absolute that belongs to the mathematical theory of infinity. The absolute was introduced into mathematical theory by Georg Cantor when he created set theory. He understood the absolute as what we are able to mathematically define, but we cannot express as a concept within set theory. The absolute has its mathematical definition, but we are lacking a mathematical proof of its existence. Badiou claims that Cantor had attempted to mathematize something that cannot be mathematized. Following Cantor, he conceives of the absolute as a place where we find all forms of multiplicities. However, it itself cannot be a multiplicity. It's a place where the mathematical theory of multiplicities is established, but it escapes the theory of multiplicities because it isn't its object. In mathematics, they later began to draw the logical distinction between a set and a class. The set corresponds to a multiplicity, whereas the class is a term that expresses that which is infinite but not a multiplicity.[4]

In *The Immanence of Truths*, Badiou primarily deals with the mathematical conception of the absolute, and he understands the absolute as an idea, even though we will see that the idea is not a synonym for the absolute. At first glance, we can think of the mathematical absolute as infinity, which is actualized in worlds that often differ fundamentally from one another, but it is not fully contained in any world. Badiou uses mathematical terminology and writes about the absolute as an absolute place—and here he allows the word place to retain its usual meaning. It is also a point in a certain world where the absolute is discovered.

As an example of the absolute place, Badiou cites the geometry of conic sections, which was created by Apollonius of Perga, a Hellenistic mathematician from the 3rd century BCE. At that time, there was no theory in physics or astronomy that utilized the forms that Apollonius expressed mathematically: the ellipse, the hyperbola, and the parabola. Although Apollonius used the parabola in studying optics when he was investigating the focal point of parabolic mirrors, he had no idea of the immense potential his discovery had. In ancient astronomy, Ptolemy's idea of the circular motion of planets prevailed. It would take twenty centuries before Apollonius's discovery of the ellipse would be used by Kepler, Copernicus, and those who followed them as an eccentric form that expresses planetary motion. His geometry of conic sections also found application in ballistics when calculating the trajectories of missiles, in rocket engineering, in astronautics, and in the creation of parabolic satellite antennas (dishes). As Badiou puts it, Apollonius discovered forms of the multiplicity of being whose possibilities were only experimentally verified after many centuries. Modern astronomy, rocket engineering, astronautics, modern satellite systems, and much more—these are all multiplicities whose forms relate to the geometry of conic sections, whose infinite potential no one knew for centuries. The forms mentioned here belong to various worlds, but they relate to Apollonius's discovery as their absolute ontological referent, which Badiou terms an absolute place and assigns the symbol *V* to it. This refers to the concept of the Void as well as to the concept of Truths (*Vérités*).[5]

In his description of the absolute place, Badiou uses the Aristotelian conceptual pair of possibility and realization, but gives it the meaning that emerges from his "Platonism of multiplicity." The absolute place is a "great void" if we look at it as the realization of one possibility or another. However, at the same time, it's also a place from which we can think about the infinity of potential forms of being that are tied to it. The Apollonian geometry of conic sections is a "great void" if we only look for a form of the laws and knowledge from modern astronomy in it, or the model of the satellite dish or the calculation of a missile's trajectory. At the place where this absolute appears, we cannot know whether it is the absolute and what form the scientific laws, inventions, technologies, and other forms of being that will one day be derived from it will have. It's not a veil of ignorance that obscures the hidden possibilities that lie within like embryos, which gradually grow into new forms of being. So how does the infinity of these possible forms exist in the absolute place? Badiou encounters the boundaries of natural language, which has an insufficient conceptual repertoire for expressing the relationship between the absolute place as a "great void" and the forms of being, which have this place as their referent. In natural language, we do not find a term that accurately captures the relationship between, let's say, modern astronomy and the Apollonian geometry of conic sections. Badiou writes that the absolute place *contains* an infinity of possible forms of being, but this statement is only true by analogy and not factually. In the period when the geometry of conic sections was discovered, this claim didn't make any sense, but the property of "making sense" isn't decisive. The way in which infinity contains possible forms of being can be captured by mathematics, and as Badiou adds, "mathematics is not the locus of sense."[6]

Let's consider another aspect of the absolute place. The individual elements of infinity that we can ascribe to it are elements that in our example correspond to Newtonian physics and astronomy, or to the construction of parabolic antennas. However, each of these elements is itself a certain infinite set. Newtonian physics contains a potential infinity of things relating to it: observations, books, statements, references, and so on. Badiou expresses this character of the absolute, which he refers to as "hyper-infinity," through mathematical theories of classes of infinities. The relationship between these classes approaches Spinoza's conception of substance, attributes, and modes. It's possible to conceive of classes of infinities as attributes of substance that have a particular property that defines them. We can understand Spinoza's modes as individual occurrences of attributes that are like an intellectual prefiguring of the sets that represent all the individual and finite elements in the world that belong to the given attribute.[7] Badiou uses Spinoza's ontology as a model that helps us better understand the relationships between individual types of infinities that have their precise expression in the mathematical theory of large cardinals. The absolute is a hyper-infinity that is immanent in individual classes of infinities and in their subsets. The hyper-infinity corresponds to the role that Spinoza gives to substance, the individual class of infinity corresponds to the attribute, and its subset corresponds to the mode. Badiou uses Spinoza's ontology as a first conception of the immanent infinity in modern philosophy, which defines the absolute differently than Christian theology does. According to Badiou, Spinoza conceived of God as an absolute without transcendence, in which there exist differences between the infinite and the finite.[8]

However, Badiou's hyper-infinity differs from Spinoza's conception of the substance because hyper-infinity is a place that appears inside a certain world—in the way that, for example, the geometry of conic sections occurred in the world of Hellenistic Greece. Although this world has the form of infinity because it is composed of multiplicities that have other multiplicities as their elements, these multiplicities of multiplicities make up an infinity of another kind than absolute infinity. Spinoza's substance contains the infinity of everything that exists, whereas Badiou's absolute contains attributes of truth, which appear in various worlds. The absolute does not include the infinity of everything that exists, as is the case with Spinoza's substance, but it contains possible truths as potentially infinite sets of elements that create truth procedures. If we were to understand the absolute as a substance in the sense of something that is all-encompassing, we would come to the conclusion that the absolute is immanent in it, which doesn't belong to the truth procedure, and thus the difference between truths and individual worlds disappears. In other words, the immanence of the absolute would be in everything, and therefore there would be truth in everything, even though Badiou understands truths as non-identical with individual worlds; rather, they are a "superfluous" element that represents an exception.

In her otherwise inspiring interpretation of Spinoza's role in *The Immanence of Truths*, Jana Beránková does not entirely clearly distinguish Spinoza's substance as a totality from Badiou's conception of the absolute. She claims that Badiou accepts Spinoza's conception of the substance as totality and differs only in understanding the totality as "not-all;" that is, as a structure that contains that which exceeds the structure and makes it impossible to create a whole. The totality exists as "not-all" because it is limited by the void.[9] This interpretation assumes that the absolute is a totality in the sense of Spinoza's all-encompassing substance, but Badiou labels the absolute place as to *V*; that is, the great void, so it is not limited by the void, but is this void itself, and it contains truths as possible forms of multiplicities in individual worlds. Badiou expresses it like this: the aim is to "establish the immanence of the absolute in the guise of singular truths."[10] This is the absolute in relation to truths that exist in worlds as exceptions, so the absolute doesn't contain all forms of multiple being in the literal sense, but only includes those forms that belong to truths that are either actual or potential.

The Relationship of the Absolute and Truths: Participation and Difference

Badiou uses the branched mathematical apparatus of contemporary theory of infinity to study the relationship between the absolute and truths. He mainly focuses on the Mostowski collapsing lemma and Łoś's theorem. In this extremely demanding mathematical apparatus, he found a way to describe the complex relationships between the absolute and truths. In the history of philosophy, these relationships were characterized in two basic ways: as the "expression" that Spinoza writes about, where he claims the attribute "expresses" a substance, or, alternately, as the "participation" (methexis) that Plato tells us exists between things and an idea.[11] If we adhere to Plato's dual determination of the relationship between things and the idea, which is both participation and also a dividing line or distance (chorismos), in Badiou's conception, we can find a similar distinction of two types of relationships, which are participation and difference. Badiou thinks through these relationships between truths and the absolute with the help of the mathematical theory of infinity, and he creates a new conception that is not merely an interpretation of Plato and Spinoza.

In examining the participatory relationship between truths and the absolute, Badiou does not conceive of truth as class *M*, which belongs to the absolute *V* as its attribute. It's a class in the sense of the mathematical category denoting infinity, which cannot be expressed as a set. The truth as an infinity belongs to another infinity, which is the absolute. The absolute *V* is an infinity that's higher than the other types of infinities, and with it we begin to "breath the air of the inaccessible peak, or rather of the immense Himalayan plateau."[12]

Badiou conceives of truth as an infinity that is lower in the hierarchy of infinities than the absolute. The absolute *V* is "embedded" into the truth expressed as class *M*. Badiou uses the symbol *j* for embedding (*plongement*) *V* into *M*. However, it is true that "every set x that 'belongs' to V there must correspond a set j(x) that 'belongs' to the class M."[13] This is not a quantitative comparison of elements that belong to *V* with elements that belong to *M*, because we do not encounter sets here, but rather classes whose massiveness cannot be compared using the means of mathematical sets, such as the subset that expresses the number of elements that belong to each of the two sets at the same time. Badiou calls this unquantifiable relationship between the absolute and truth a "great proximity" between *V* and *M*.[14] It's about accurately expressing the property of "being almost like" or "resembling," which are not entirely transferable to the relationship of "being an element." The basic logical relations of "being an element" and "being a subset" are necessary here to replace relations that are similar to them but express relationships between classes and not between subsets. This difficulty especially manifests itself in the question of how to formulate the fact that attributes as truths are at the same time both universal (they're generic multiplicities and they act in many worlds) and particular (they're composed from the material of the given world and belong to themselves). Thus, truths are not absolute, but are almost absolute.

The particularity of truths is captured in the mathematical apparatus with the concept of transitivity. Truth is illustrated by class *M*, which is transitive. This means that any element *x* that is an element of *M* is also a subset of *M*. This class is "closed," constituting a "world of its own within V."[15] Each element of class *M* is therefore also an element of *M*, and so on. Badiou uses Mostowski's lemma in order to express the relationship between *M* and *V*, which will correspond to the relationship of "being an element of," which is expressed with the symbol

$\ulcorner$.[16] In its simplified form, Mostowski's lemma says that it is possible to create class *C*, which is structured by the relationship called a well-founded extensional relation (whose symbol is *R*). This is the relation between *M* and *V* (between a truth and the absolute), and for class *M* it can replace the relation of "being an element of." This is possible because the structure (*C*, *R*) and the structure (*M*, $\ulcorner$) are uniquely isomorphic, so there is a structural identity between them.[17] Thus, thanks to Mostowski's lemma, Badiou can claim that *M* belongs to *V* as its element, even though *M* and *V* are classes and not sets. The infinity *M* (truth) is therefore possible to understand as an element or attribute of another infinity, which is *V*. A truth is thus an infinity that is particular because it is a transitive class, while at the same time it's also universal because the truth participates in the absolute as its element with the relation "being an element of" expressed through Mostowski's lemma.

Badiou expresses the relationship between a truth and the absolute as proximity. His conception of proximity enables the distinction of degrees of proximity to the absolute and doesn't introduce a dualistic gap between them in the way Plato's chorismos does.[18] Badiou introduced into his ontology the concept of the ultrafilter, or more precisely, "under the barbaric name of κ-complete non-principal ultrafilter," as the crucial concept in contemporary theory of infinity.[19] The ultrafilter is formulated in a theorem that was published in the mid-1950s by Jerzy Łoś, and in set theory, it is related to the relationship between two sets. This relationship, which is relation (*R*), defines the arrangement of the elements of these sets. For example, the relation "being larger" arranges the elements in such a way that one element from one set is assigned to an element of a second set that is larger than it is (thus creating binary pairs). If we have set *X* arranged through the relation *R*, the filter indicates the subset *Y*, which, with respect to relation *R*, fulfills a certain property (this is the "downward directed set *X*").[20] An ultrafilter refers to the relation between the set *X* and its potential set *P*(*X*), which is a set of all their subsets. An ultrafilter is a non-empty subset of the set *P*(*X*), which has a certain property (it's again a downward directed set).

Badiou provides an example that serves only to assist a basic understanding of the ultrafilter, but not understanding the meaning of the absolute. We have the statement "if we do not take into account significant, though brief revolutionary moments, France will be dominated by a primarily conservative or reactionary ideology." This statement does not claim that all the French are conservative or that they agree with reactionary ideology, but it says that nearly all of the French are like this and assumes that there are certain exceptions. From the perspective of the theory of multiplicities, we can reformulate it so that France is, let's say, between the year 1915 and the present, a multiplicity of mentalities, impulses, expressions, newspaper articles, television discussions, and debates in cafes. Then it can be claimed that a very large part of the "France" set consists of elements that are conservative or reactionary. This very large part is nearly identical to the infinite set, but not entirely identical to it. It is a part that is defined by the ultrafilter on the "France" set. The ultrafilter is an apparatus that makes it possible to claim that a certain statement about nearly all the elements of the set being a certain way as assigned by the predicate ("being conservative or reactionary") is an acceptable approximation of what is true about the entire set and what we cannot know. The set marked as "France" is too extensive, and moreover, it's impossible to establish verbal expressions, activities, and debates on this subject for all French people who lived from 1815 to the present. An ultrafilter works by defining the subset of a set based on a particular predicate ("France"), and we can claim that a statement about this set ("France is conservative or reactionary") is almost true. As Badiou emphasizes, this example is a certain caricature of the theory of truths, because France, defined as an infinite set of mentalities, impulses, expressions, and so on, "by itself has no ontological dignity or even existence" and doesn't correspond to "what happens when truths are involved."[21] However, the reader who is not a specialized mathematician is able to get an idea of the fundamental significance Łoś's theorem has had in Badiou's ontology. Badiou interprets it as follows: "any statement (implicitly related to *V*) is equivalent to a statement in which the 'absolute' existence of a term is replaced with its approximate existence, in the sense of the approximation by an ultrafilter as presented above."[22]

We can also show the effect of the ultrafilter in another example from Badiou. Suppose we have a set *E* with certain functions, which is a subset of the set *V*. For instance, the function of set *E* is politics of emancipation. It originates in one place, but it is always addressed to all humanity, including all the living and the dead (Badiou is referring to Comte's famous saying that "humanity is always made up of more dead than living"). In this example, the whole of humanity is the set *V*, which represents the "absolute referent" of this international emancipatory politics. It creates a set *E* composed of various elements that are also determined by local culture. The whole of humanity does not represent the absolute in the meaning that Badiou gives this word in his philosophy of the absolute, but it's a metaphor of the absolute as in the case of the "France" set, which helps us understand the meaning of ultrafilters. The function of "conducting an international emancipatory politics" creates an ultrafilter for the set E, which enables the organization of international operations or the creation of an "Internationale" with the participation of revolutionaries from various countries and different cultures. This international emancipatory politics is a function of the set E in relation to set V, which comprises the whole of humanity. We now have a class of all the individual international politics in various countries and different cultures. These politics will not be the same, but at the same time they won't be so different that they become entirely particular. Thanks to the ultrafilter called the "Internationale," we can claim that these politics will be *almost* identical. Badiou expresses their relationship as a certain mathematical abstraction. There are two functions f and g (two policies that are not identical), and they are the functions E in relation to V. These functions are almost identical when for all x, that are elements of the set E, the function f and the function g have the same value, which they acquire because they are part of E, which is in the ultrafilter. Thus, these functions are not identical, but they have the same value given to them by belonging to the ultrafilter, which in Badiou's example is the "Internationale." Both of these functions are a drawing close to the identity that exists as the "Idea," which is an international emancipatory politics.[23]

In this example, we find that the participation of truths in the absolute or the idea is not participation in an identity that we could precisely define. The different functions of E, which are nearly identical, represent different truth procedures relating to one event. Their identity, that is, some ideal type of "international emancipatory politics," cannot be deduced from the event itself or from this or that truth procedure that this event develops. (As stated in the passage dedicated to Badiou's concept of the truth procedure, there isn't any "correct" truth procedure that would serve as a criterion of correctness for the other truth procedures.) This identity exists in the absolute or in the idea as a form of possible being, which, however, cannot be precisely defined. We do not have immediate access to it because this identity doesn't exist as something given. We only have the ultrafilter apparatus, which enables the establishment of the degree of proximity between individual procedures and this undefinable identity that exists in the absolute or in the idea. Through the ultrafilter, we can then claim that a certain truth "touches" the absolute (via participation, expression, similarity, etc.). Badiou also uses the term "place of absolutization of a truth" to express this relationship.[24]

Thus far, we have dealt with the relationship of participation between truth and the absolute. Now it is necessary to examine in what way truth differs from the absolute. The difference between truth and the absolute arises from the fact that the material from which the truth procedure is composed is particular because it's connected with a certain specific historical situation. For the sake of simplicity, I'll only consider one truth and not multiple truths, which relate to the various functions of the set E. Due to its composition, which is made up of a particular material from the given situation, it doesn't have an immediate relationship to the absolute. It does not present itself as belonging to the absolute in the sense of $E \in V$. Its relation to the absolute has a derived form, which Badiou expresses as $j(E) \in M$. E is the set determined by functions that define the effect of truth in a given situation. This is an embedding of the absolute, as symbolized by $j(E)$. E is an element of M as an infinite class that belongs to a given truth. This, as a set of elements of a given local procedure, shows a particular and final character. The infinite class M defined in this way is what brings about the absolutization of truth, but the truth as a creative procedure is not a copy of the absolute but is always separated from the absolute. Badiou proves that the absolute remains separate from a truth in which it is expressed (Spinoza) or in which it participates (Plato).[25] Here, we encounter Badiou's conception of a dialectic of participation that consists in "ontological identity and localized difference."[26] The truth develops in a certain final situation in which a temporal relationship arises with the absolute which, figuratively speaking, props it up. The absolute diversifies in individual situations and worlds through locally and temporally limited truths. As Badiou says, this takes place according to Hegel's fine phrase that the absolute is "with us."[27] These ideas are essential for understanding the dialectic of participation and difference. According to Badiou, the absolute is related to the locally developed truth, which becomes one of its attributes without this truth losing its particular uniqueness. This relationship between the absolute and an individual truth forms the orientation of "human animals," which exist as subjects of truth. This orientation has a tension within it that arises because there is a difference between the absolute and singular truths that is brought about by the randomness of truth procedures.[28] Truth is not a dead equivalent to the absolute. However, on the other hand, the absolute exists as that which is more than truth.

Two Meanings of the Idea

The dialectic of participation and difference that takes place between the absolute and a truth allows Badiou to introduce a new meaning of the idea.

Badiou usually uses the term "idea" as a Platonic name for the absolute, as testified by his statement that "the absolute place, for Plato, is the realm of the Ideas."[29] However, it suggests the idea of another meaning that isn't identical to the concept of the absolute. The place for this specific meaning of the idea arises from the fact that the absolute is inconsistent in itself, because between the absolute and a truth, there exists an identity expressed as $j(x)$, that is, as a set that belongs to the absolute and at the same time to truth, which is an expression of the embedding of the absolute into the truth. Truth participates in the absolute, but at the same time, as we have seen above, it develops in ways that prevent it from being a trivial copying of the absolute. It is not an imprint of the set $j(x)$ into specific conditions of a given situation. The embedding of the absolute into a truth, therefore, indicates that the absolute itself is inconsistent. The idea, then, does not coincide with the absolute place, but it is a certain form of relationship between the absolute place and a truth, which is created through the embedding of the absolute into a truth.[30] The idea represents a form of infinity that increases. The absolute "embeds" into one truth, but then into more truths, which appear in unpredictable ways in other situations. The idea is a form of embedding that expresses the relationship between the infinite absolute and the infinite class M, which, as a truth, is an attribute of the absolute. The idea is also a relationship between the absolute and another infinite class M, which is this attribute in another world. Badiou says that "an idea always takes stock of an earlier idea."[31] However, there is not a cumulative ascension of multiplicities (such as knowledge, experience, and visions) that would lead to an idea that represents the last infinity, which already contains all the possibilities through which the absolute "embeds" into truths. Badiou refers to Kunen's theorem, which suggests that there is no ultimate form of infinity in which the ascending procession of the already known types culminates.[32]

I interpret Badiou's understanding of the idea such that the idea has its basic meaning that corresponds to the concept of the absolute, and it also has its second meaning, in which the idea expresses the potential infinity of past, present, and future embeddings of the absolute into truths in individual worlds. It follows that there cannot be a claim made that any embedding of the absolute into truth is going to be the last one. In other words, no previous realization of a truth as an absolute of the absolute exhausts all the possibilities through which the absolute "embeds" into truths. Thus, it does not exhaust the idea in the meaning of "embedding," because the idea, in this sense, is infinite. Therefore, Badiou conceives of the idea as an "infinite anticipation as to the existence, to be confirmed in reality, of a possibly generic universe."[33] He develops this idea using

Scott and Jensen's theorem, which proves the existence of a non-constructible infinity.[34] It is an infinity that cannot be defined by the construction of any mathematical model. According to Badiou, the idea is a non-constructible infinity that escapes all counting operations that would translate it into a result that follows from what we know. It is an infinity that escapes every type of mathematical expression. As Badiou says, these qualities show the "power of the Idea" even in a period that considers finiteness as the last horizon of the present time.[35] We can therefore relate these formulations of Badiou's to the interregnum, in which truths have ceased to operate. They show that the interregnum is a world in which, nevertheless, or perhaps precisely because of it, we encounter the power of the Idea.

Badiou's Atheism and the Hypothesis of a Materialistic God

Due to possible misunderstandings, it should be noted that Badiou doesn't understand the absolute in the religious sense of the word: his position is strictly atheist. He considers religion to be a narrative or a fable that doesn't belong among the four types of truth, even though it offers a pattern of faith, fidelity, and the subject that are analogous to their form in the domains of the four types of truth.[36] However, Badiou says there is no effective refutation of religious belief because the God of religion is the object of narration, which isn't possible to object to. It is narrative that the believer desires, and it doesn't have the character of rational knowledge. Badiou considers the God of religion to be a story that is credible to millions of people, so it's necessary to acknowledge it as a sui generis phenomenon that we cannot discuss in the same way as we would discuss a set of rational claims.[37] However, he polemicizes against theology as a doctrine of a transcendent God. Theology connected with monotheistic religion understands the absolute as a being that is transcendent and stands over the finite world. According to this theology, conceiving the absolute as part of our world is an unacceptable manifestation of pride. According to Badiou, the idea that everything in our world is finite is the central motif of oppression, which aims to suppress every conviction that works are created in our world whose core is the "immanence of infinity."[38] The religious suppression of the immanence of infinity represents one of the four forms of repression that "grounds" emancipatory ambitions as mere manifestations of finiteness. The transcendent conception of the absolute fills a similar ideological function as the state, economics, and the philosophy of finiteness, each of which in its own way suppresses the presence of the absolute in this world. Badiou thus overturns the idea that the radically emancipatory trends of the nineteenth and twentieth centuries, such as Marxism, represented a secularization of religion. From Badiou's conception of infinity, it can be deduced that modern emancipatory trends are actually a secularism of the absolute that opposes religion, the state, economics, and the philosophy of finiteness, which suppress the existence of the absolute in this world. Secularism in its philosophical sense expresses the view that we interpret life, society, and history only according to principles that are part of our world, without appealing to a religious interpretation in which God acts as a principle that transcends our world. If we find the absolute in this world, which is not transcendent but instead is immanent, this is a secular absolute. Therefore, Badiou's position can be called a secularism of the absolute.

Badiou, however, finds yet another meaning of the concept of God, and this one isn't connected with the suppression of the immanent infinity. Although he refuses God's monopoly on infinity, as this is expressed in monotheistic religious texts, he says that we can understand God as a name that refers to truth in the plural through "the imaginary of the religious narratives."[39] Badiou draws on Lacan's idea that "God is unconscious," and turns it around so that God becomes "the unconscious itself." God is a symbolic name connected with an *imaginary* narrative in our consciousness, which is able to shatter this imaginary narrative or at least limit its effects, and we encounter a reality that is outside of our consciousness. In this way, we discover "a capacity that we were unaware of in ourselves."[40] Badiou is thinking about God in this way as a cipher of truths that the subject doesn't have under its control and which it can never fully contain in its consciousness, because the subject is merely a local instance of the infinite truth procedure. The unconscious is "the internal transcendence of the conscious mind, i.e., the immanent distance at which the conscious mind can draw from reserves over which it has no control but which exist nonetheless."[41]

Badiou therefore turns around the concept of God as a transcendent absolute that forbids the appearance of an imminent infinity in the finite world. God becomes a cipher of immanent infinity that operates in the domain of the unconscious as a reality that disrupts our consciousness by opening a gap in it that separates it from truths. Badiou transforms God's external transcendence from the world into an internal transcendence of truths from the subject. God means an imaginary sign for the way truths operate. However, could we reverse this model so that God becomes a symbol that isn't imaginary but real; that is, the kind of symbol that with its structure expresses the real infinity that Badiou writes about? If God is merely an imaginary symbol, it means that it can be replaced with a symbol or concept that is real in the sense that it captures the character of infinity as real. The absolute or the idea represents such a concept. I then argue that God can be conceived as a symbol that cannot be replaced with another symbol, because it expresses the reality of infinity, or more specifically, it denotes the character of infinity, which the concept of the absolute or the idea cannot capture.

First of all, it's necessary to consider whether from the perspective of the radical orthodox theologians (e.g., Milbank) or Badiou's interpretation of the traditional conception of God as a transcendental absolute tied to Scott's univocity of being, which with its consequences separates the sphere of the divine and the earthly and introduces an opposition between the finite and the infinite. In the conception of radical orthodoxy, God does not entirely correspond to Badiou's interpretation of a transcendent God as Scott's infinity, which is the opposite of the finiteness of this world. As stated in the subchapter "The domain of theology: radical orthodoxy," the radical orthodox theologians conceive of God as a processual movement of difference, symbolized by the Trinity, which is how he participates with his being in the affairs of this world. Here we can mention their idea that finite being participates in infinite being, which enables the finite to contain a certain aspect of the infinite through the "analogia entis." However, the objection can be raised that the finite is infinite only to the extent that it is dependent on the transcendent infinite, and thus it is not an immanent infinity in the true sense of the word.

However, we can understand God as a form of the absolute's being that is shared with individual absolute places. In Badiou's four types of truth, there exists something shared, although it has a shared form determined by the corresponding domain of the truth's occurrence. Badiou develops a general theory of the absolute, truth, and the subject that are diversified according to whether the absolute, truth, and subject are in the political domain, the domain of art, and so on. These truths are always situated in a particular world. My hypothesis of a materialistic God consists in God being a common form of absolutes, truths, and subjects that exist in a plurality of their individual occurrences. Badiou developed a general theory of these formations, so we can ask what the relationship is between these formations and their general description and form, and what they look like in the domains of politics, art, science, and love. In what way do these generally formatted formations exist, if we know that they don't occur in a purely abstract form in the world, but always as this or that work in the domain of science (Apollonius's discovery of the geometry of conic sections), as a work of art (Pessoa's poem), as a political work (the October Revolution), or as a work of love? The relations between the absolute, truths, and the subject are always thus concrete in individual worlds and do not take the form of relations between these formations in their abstract form. So how do the absolute, the truth, and the subject exist as abstract concepts? We can certainly say that they exist as theoretical objects of investigation in Badiou's writing. The individual occurrences of absolutes, truths, and subjects have something in common, and Badiou investigates it as his theoretical objects. However, isn't there a concept here that would express that the political absolute, the artistic absolute, and so on, have something in common?

My hypothesis is that what they have in common can be expressed with the symbol of God. This hypothesis is inspired not only by Badiou, but also by Paul Tillich, who conceived of God as a form of being that exists as the deepest layer or "depth" of human artistic, scientific, and ethical activity. As a theologian, Tillich is somewhat too existentialist when he understands the "depth" that appears in all these diverse human activities as the "ultimate concern." In the field of ethics, he claims that this depth manifests as an unconditional bindingness of the moral imperative; in science, it has the nature of a passionate desire for knowledge; in art, it has the form of a longing to express the last meaning.[42] However, Tillich's idea that God is a symbol that expresses that which cannot be symbolized is fundamental for my hypothesis. This unsymbolizable element is the experience of infinite being or being that disrupts the limited experience of ourselves as persons.[43] The unsymbolizable element of God can be interpreted as the real, which disrupts our imaginary images of the world, which are the contents of our consciousness. According to Tillich, God is a symbol that arises from the collective unconscious, in which there exists the experience of infinite being.[44]

If we leave aside Tillich's overly religious terminology ("the holiness of the ultimate being"), these considerations can provide us with a guideline for how to formulate the hypothesis of a God that can be derived from Badiou's philosophy. This is the *hypothesis of a materialist God*. Like Badiou, Tillich claims that God operates like the unconscious. In his conception, this symbol expresses the experience of infinite being as being that appears in the "depth" of human activity. Tillich connects this experience with that which touches us most deeply and to which no symbol, not even the symbol of God, corresponds. This symbol is internally split: it includes the reality of that which cannot be symbolized and that which disrupts the integrity of a given symbol. In Badiou's terminology, this symbol of God is that which is not counted as one. Tillich's ideas show that God is not an infinite being, which is the foundation of human artistic, scientific, or political activities, but it also isn't the "One" as a transcendent absolute. Infinite being is present in these activities in the form of the unconscious, which is able to limit or break down ideas about art, science, ethics, and politics that are connected with human finiteness. God is the infinite unconscious being that operates in various types of activity, but at the same time manifests itself in them as that which all these activities have in common in their depths. Tillich calls this common element, for example, the "power of being."

According to my hypothesis, Badiou's understanding of God can be turned around on the basis of Tillich's impulses in such a way that it is a form of being of absolutes, truths, and subjects that is analogous to Tillich's conception of infinite being, which exists as the basis of individual types of activities. Although God continues to express the inner transcendence of a certain truth (for instance, artistic truth) in relation to the subject, this transcendence is external in a certain sense because it also concerns the other types of truths (for instance, political and scientific truths and the truth of love) in their occurrences, which are somehow doubly outside of the subject's control. The artistic subject is a local instance of a certain artistic truth procedure, but besides this, its form of existence has something in common with the scientific subject, the political subject, and the subject of love: the form of being that is "being a subject." Therefore, these different truths also apply to the artistic subject in some way. This subject has only locally limited control over the corresponding truth procedure for art, but of course, as a subject of art, it doesn't have any control over the other types of truth procedures. This is why I speak about these procedures being doubly outside of the subject's control. As an artistic subject, Picasso has a certain control over the local development of the truth procedure called cubism, but he has no control over the developing procedure of the October Revolution, even though Picasso is actually an example of an artist who was aware of the affinity of both truth procedures (cubism and the October Revolution), as is evident from his communist convictions.

In Badiou's conception of the subject, the infinite (truth as an attribute of the absolute) coexists with the finite as the material of the local development of the truth procedure. According to the proposed hypothesis, the subject is a form of being that, through its local participation in the infinity of a certain truth, participates in what I call the materialist God. This is because the subject, by participating in a particular truth (cubism, the October Revolution), takes on a form of being that is common to all subjects who are participating in this way, and it's this common form of being that I term the materialist God. It's impossible to directly express the common form of being through concepts or symbols because these are connected with the domains in which individual absolutes, truths, and subjects appear. The expressions are only analogous, like when we find a special element in one of Picasso's pictures that is a trace or "touch" of infinite being. The trace of infinity in a particular work points to the materialist God, whose different traces we can then discover in the political domain of truths, the scientific domain, and the domain of love based on the analogy of the trace in the image. These references can lead to our understanding the already discovered trace of infinite being in, for example, the domain of truths in art being understood in terms of its traces in science or in love. In this way, we transform the meaning of the political truth, where we discover the trace of the materialist God who has something in common with art, science, or love.

The materialistic God as a common form of infinite being of individual absolutes and truths is an unconsciousness from which emerge impulses to discover that the subject participating in the development of one truth is thus indirectly contributing to the development of the other truth procedures, even though it is not influencing these procedures as their operator. A simple example from art history is the changes in various artistic genres that took place during the period of the French Revolution. The political subject connected with the truth of the French Revolution created conditions that brought about changes in the domain of art, and even in the domains of science and love. Badiou's conception of the subject has a kind of theological foreshadowing in the figure of Christ, even though the author himself does not refer to this foreshadowing. The figure of Christ contains a "divine dimension" because it participates in the infinite being of the Trinity while at the same time animal human properties operate within him and create his finiteness (e.g., he experiences mortal anxiety and sweats blood in the Garden of Gethsemane). On the basis of this foreshadowing, we can consider that the subject relates to an individual truth procedure and to a particular absolute, but in this way, it also relates to the materialistic God that exists in the individual truths and absolutes. Its form of being therefore shows a similar structure to the figure of Christ.

The hypothesis of a materialist God can be further developed through further impulses that we can find in philosophers and theologians who deal with the existence of the infinite in our world, such as Ernst Bloch and Pierre Teilhard de Chardin. Here, I limit myself to the assertion that Badiou's book *The Immanence of Truths* provides the possibility of deriving the hypothesis of a materialist God as a symbolic expression of a common form of being that is diversified into individual absolutes, truths, subjects, and works in an infinite number of possible worlds.

Fidelity to an Idea and the Decentered Position of Philosophy: Solving Mysteries

In "A sketch of an ethics," a chapter of *The Immanence of Truths*, Badiou sets out three interrelated imperatives.

The first is: *Commit to an Idea*. It is necessary to commit to an Idea in order to oppose the basic imperative of the contemporary world, which tells us "Live without any Ideas!". This imperative expresses the dominance of finiteness in the period of the interregnum, which represses emancipatory thinking. According to Badiou, the doctrine of finiteness obscures the Idea by referring to the fact of our living in a period after the death of ideology. Committing to an Idea means that we shape our existence according to a certain non-constructible infinity and we are adamant in this. Eventually, an "encounter with the generic" may occur.[45]

The second imperative says: *You must contribute to uncovering;* that is, it's necessary to take part in the uncovering of the existence of the infinite. By this, Badiou has in mind actions that benefit an Idea, through which we intervene in a given situation and find a point at which the numbing veil of infinity starts to dissolve. If we believe that the Idea can live, even in our ordinary lives, the possibility of another life opens up, despite the world of the interregnum in which the ideology of finiteness dominates.

The third imperative is: *Open thought up to real infinity*. This imperative connects the two previous ones. Badiou elaborates on it in this way: stick with an Idea and be strong so that we don't allow it to be obscured, which means, in individual cases, we begin to liberate ourselves from the domination of the finite. As a result of this, we will make a creation out of part of our life, and it will be a creation marked by infinity, which will no longer be covered.[46] The work in which "touches" of the infinite appear in this way will be a testimony to the reality of the infinite.

In these imperatives, we find an answer to the mysteries that accompany the entire investigation of Badiou's philosophy from the perspective of the interregnum: What position does philosophy have if it cannot relate to truths as its conditions? What can one be faithful to in an interregnum situation after the closing of truth procedures? Badiou's imperatives offer a surprisingly clear answer to these mysteries. In the interregnum, there exists the possibility of a fidelity that doesn't immediately relate to the Truth, but rather to the Idea. It is fidelity to the Idea that has a somewhat different character than fidelity to the Truth. An Idea, in the basic meaning of the non-constructible infinite, contains within it a balance of the previous ideas or previous forms of this idea, but it's not a balance or final accounting of it. The idea is a non-constructible infinity doesn't close in this way. The sequence of truths ended in the 1980s and closed as generic procedures that have their historical subjects. However, Ideas continue to exist as infinities of possible forms of being that have not been exhausted by their previous embodiments. "Commit to an Idea" therefore doesn't mean connecting to a certain form of being that had appeared at another time, as is the case with fidelity to a truth. Badiou formulates his imperatives for a situation in which the existence of truths and ideas is questioned to such a degree that truths and ideas act as metaphysical chimeras or cultural constructs. In particular, the first imperative of "Commit to an Idea" and the third imperative "Open thought up to real infinity" are sufficiently eloquent in portraying the interregnum situation in which it is first necessary to create the intellectual space in which truth and the idea appear as phenomena that are really operating in history. The second imperative "You must contribute to uncovering" is meant to evoke the emergence of a space of action in which a "work" that bears the traces of infinity begins to be embodied. In this space of thought and action, the ideological idea of the nonexistence of truths and ideas begins to dissolve. This is thus about the existence of truths as such as well as the establishment of real possibilities for a new beginning.

Fidelity to an Idea differs from fidelity to a Truth in its historical form of individual truths in particular domains because it affirms its very existence in the space of thought and action. By contrast, fidelity to the Truth is connected with operations by a subject that connects certain elements of a given situation to an event. Fidelity to the Idea expressed by the above-mentioned imperatives follows Badiou's ethical formulations from his earlier books. For example, in the book *The Meaning of Sarkozy*, he writes that in our oppressive interval phase, it is first necessary to strive for the "communist hypothesis" to even exist. This is done through a combination of emancipatory ideas that are globally universal and political experiments that are local but have universal potential. In this way, it is possible to contribute to the communist hypothesis beginning to operate "in consciousness and in concrete situations."[47] In the interregnum, it is possible to carry out experiments in the domains of politics, art, and love that are combined with ideas that form the basic condition for the new existence of truths. From Badiou's statements, it turns out that fidelity to the Idea consists in a dialectic between consciousness and experimentation. It's an awareness that opens up to universal ideas in which there is a touch of the infinite. This consciousness is found in a two-way relationship with experimental practice, which is not connected with a particular historical event as its procedure because it took place in the interregnum. It is experimentation that may eventually prove to be a dead end, or perhaps instead it will be retrospectively considered a condition for the emergence of a new event or even as an event itself. In the interregnum situation, the most proximate goal is creating a space of thought and action in which the traces of infinity begin to appear in the form of experiments that dissolve its numbing shroud. Fidelity to an Idea thus lies in the realization of this goal.

What is the position of philosophy here? At the very end of *The Immanence of Truths*, Badiou writes that the task of philosophy since its inception is: "to create, in the conditions of its time, the knowledge of the existential possibility of truth."[48] In *The Immanence of Truths*, the determination of the position of philosophy changes if we compare it with the position of the conditioning of truths, which was discussed in *Manifesto for Philosophy*. In *The Immanence of Truths*, Badiou addresses the position philosophy has in a period in which truths are not currently operating as conditioning, which relates to the domains of politics, art, and love. The currently operating truth procedures are thus only found in the domain of science (mathematics), which is why I called their position eccentric. In *The Immanence of Truths*, Badiou continues in this eccentric position, and by using the mathematics of the large cardinals, he creates philosophical concepts that concern infinity, including its types and the relations between them. Thus, a philosophy is created that offers a theory of infinity and ideas that capture an infinity greater than individual truths. It follows from this theory that after the end of the currently operating truths, the absolute and ideas that contain the possibility of a new beginning in the real world still exist. Badiou's theory of the absolute and ideas causes a certain change in the position of philosophy. Its eccentric position is centered in the relationship to all the domains in which truths have appeared. Philosophy creates imperatives that in every domain call for the activation of a dialectic between the consciousness of the infinite and experimental practice. Movements that experimentally get close to the idea and intervene in a given situation in the interregnum can happen in every domain. They thus create the conditions under which it becomes possible to arrive at the acknowledgment of the existence of ideas and truths within individual domains. Experimental practice in art, science, and love can thus begin to condition philosophy and act in the place of the truth procedures that condition philosophy in the periods when we are not in an interregnum. If Badiou writes in *Manifesto for Philosophy* about the conditioning of philosophy with truths, I deduce from his *The Immanence of Truths* that in the interregnum, philosophy is conditioned by ideas. In this way, philosophy's eccentric position becomes—to a certain extent—more centered.

We can understand the interregnum both as a period after the closing of truths and as a period in which instead of truths the absolute and ideas appear. I interpret Badiou's theory of the absolute and of ideas in relation to the situation of the interregnum, and I claim that the period of the interregnum is exceptional in one respect. In periods when the truths are operating, the subject relates to its truth procedure as its operator, and its consciousness is formed through this procedure. His consciousness is exposed first to the truth, and then through the mediation of this truth, it is also exposed to the absolute and the idea. An artist who develops a modernist artistic procedure touches the infinite idea of art by connecting this procedure with artistic elements that have appeared in entirely different worlds, such as in African tribes. An activist developing a communist political sequence primarily orients themselves according to this sequence, and not according to the absolute or an idea, even if they are creating a "work" in which Badiou's theory would describe touches of the absolute. These procedures disappear during the interregnum, and therefore the "animal human beings" that strive for emancipation from the oppressive conditions of finiteness have no other possibility than finding a form of existence that is created by fidelity to the Idea. Their consciousness is formed in relation to the Idea, and not in relation to Truth. For this reason, I argue that their consciousness and form of existence are closer to the idea than is the case with the subject of truth.

According to Badiou, the idea can be expressed as a non-constructible infinity that contains its past embeddings $j(x)$ into truths as its attributes, as well as the infinity of other possible embeddings. In the interregnum, the individual or the collective is liberated from the limits of the finite by re-presenting these previous embeddings, which are elements of the idea as infinity, in their consciousness and their experimental activity. In the interregnum conditions, an anamnesis of past truths as attributes of the infinite idea takes place. The interregnum is a situation that opens a window to the past, which was previously partially obscured by the presence of current truths. Past truths are not seen here through the lens of a current truth, but through the lens of the idea itself. Thus, an anamnesis of truths in individual domains as elements of the idea is performed against the background of their absence in the interregnum. The absence of current truths creates, in a sense, a unique relationship to the idea or to eternity. As Badiou put it, "Eternity is always the moment where history, in some sense, is without interest."[49]

In my books, I have described this relationship as an answer to radical negativity. We relate to the idea on the basis of experience of disintegrating and numbing nothingness. This act takes place in a suicidal space in which the idea begins to appear as the object of desire, which is the antithanatic answer to the experience of the closeness of real psychosomatic death.[50] I have proposed this responsive conception of ideas because, among other reasons, I believe that Badiou does not take the longing for transgression that especially manifests in the late phases of truths sufficiently into account. A desire arises to transgress ethics, which comes from a fidelity to the truth, because the truth is already in a decadent phase and its extinction is drawing near. The responsive conception of ideas is based on the fact that the near-death experience remains present and acts as a formative factor in our relationship to the idea. I understand the interregnum as a period when the absence of truths creates radical negativity, and therefore the conditions for the emergence of a new relationship to ideas arise in it. The interregnum is then a time in which an anamnesis of past truths is developed, which is responsive to the above-discussed sense. In this way, conditions are developed for the appearance of an event and of truth procedures because the transgressive nature of the desire that was formed in the period of the breakdown of truths and was carried over into the interregnum gradually disappears. The weakening of the transgressive character of desire manifests in the appearance of circulations or metamodernist oscillations in which there is a desire to transcend the transgression itself by approaching an identification with a truth, a common vision, or a collective identity. The interregnum is a time when it becomes possible to create a relationship to an idea that will not be transgressive. At the end of the period of truths, this relationship had become de facto impossible and its postmodern ironization ensued.

At the same time, ideas like infinity contain an anticipatory dimension that concerns the possibility of new truths in the future. The anticipatory dimension is first formed in relation to the past. This takes place through a series of acts of reminiscing (anamnesis) on past embeddings of the absolute into truths that provide a certain imaginal, future-focused material. If we recall the existence of truths in the past, it's not so difficult to imagine their future arrival. In my concept of the responsive theory of ideas, the anticipatory dimension also has a second source, which is the radically negative experience created by the interregnum. This experience evokes an antithanatic act, through which a certain psychological, mental, and ethical energy is created, which is anticipatory in the true sense. It turns to the formations that are the result of the experimental attempts at finding new forms of truths and provides them with a certain benchmark. If it turns out that there is no mutually evolving interplay, a tendency arises for the creation of new formations that will be better attuned to this energy. This process evokes an experimental tendency aiming toward a formation that will one day be recognized as an event, which heralds the end of the interregnum.

The Idea as an Infinite Composition of Unity and Plurality

The idea represents the infinity that manifests itself in the interregnum through its previous truths, which are oriented on the basis of fidelity to the Idea to the future as an anticipation of a new truth. If we commit to an Idea, a certain unifying form appears, which has a paradoxical structure. It's a form that appears as a non-constructible infinity that cannot be expressed as a set of elements. The idea itself stands outside of the possibility of counting it as one within the framework of set theory. In Badiou's philosophy, set theory is a tool he uses in describing our world (the situation, the state, the event, truth, the subject, logics of worlds). In Badiou's conception, the idea is formulated within the framework of the theory of large cardinal numbers and it corresponds to the category of the class. From the perspective of our world, described with the help of set theory, the idea is uncountable. With this reservation, however, the idea as a non-constructible infinity represents a certain unifying form. In the interregnum, the idea acts as an infinity that contains updated and potential forms of its embedding into truths. Therefore, individual truths can be considered in diverse worlds like historical updates of a certain amount of possibilities that exist in the infinity that is the idea.

In the period of the interregnum, we can distinguish individual truths from various worlds as attributes of one infinity. There are a number of truths that, according to Badiou, begin in art with prehistoric paintings in the Lascaux cave and end with the abstract painting of the twentieth century. The idea of art conceived as infinity allows us to glimpse qualities in these artworks that refer to the existence of a certain participation in one infinity, even if the works are thousands of years apart in time. These works appear as a multiplicity of forms of being, which is an updating of the part of the possibilities that exist in the idea of art as a non-constructible infinity. In the domain of politics, the idea of communism emerges, which "embeds" itself into the truths in many worlds that are separated by temporal and cultural gaps. We find certain unifying qualities in the disparate multiplicities of individual embodiments of this political idea. This infinite idea instigates a manner of seeing that makes it possible to recognize the common qualities that are found in prehistoric forms of equality in ancient tribal societies, in the Paris Commune, and in the communist sequence of the twentieth century. These long series can be supplemented with more and more elements where their participation in the idea as infinity can be distinguished. The elements in these series can fundamentally differ from one another, so from the purely phenomenal perspective, they may not have any common features at all. The case is similar with many discoveries and inventions from various periods and worlds that share the common quality of participating in Apollonius's geometry of conical sections. The elliptical model of the movement of celestial bodies and the parabolic antenna have almost nothing in common if we look at them as immediately given objects. It is only when a form of seeing is introduced by the idea of infinity that we recognize their multiplicitous participation in Apollonius's geometry, which represents their common quality. Out of these, it creates a number of elements that are open to the past and the future. In the past, it's possible to discover other formations with this quality that have thus far escaped our notice. In the future, new formations with this property may emerge, whose similarity cannot be deduced from previous formations. As stated above, this is not a cumulative series in which one element would follow upon the accumulated multiplicity connected with the previous elements and build upon them. There are gaps between the elements in this series, and they may appear so different as specific formations that they appear to be heterogeneous. Their common property is only sufficiently visible through the infinite idea that they participate in.

The Interregnum as an Uncovering of Infinity

For centuries and millennia, series of artworks, political acts and movements, scientific discoveries, and love stories have proceeded in which we can recognize "touches of the absolute." These series are visible in a period when truths are being updated, and they are seen as new elements of these truths. At that time, the subject connects itself to a certain truth and in these series it sees an element—a truth, of which it is the subject—and this truth determines the way it approaches them. In other words, a certain truth, developed in a given world, creates a way that we can recognize the other elements in the given order; that is, in a historical series of political acts and movements, in a series of scientific discoveries, or in a series of love stories. In these past series, we emphasize the similarities and differences in relation to the developed new truth as—for now—the last element of the series, and we look to it as a reference point. The current truth certainly creates a more intensive relationship to past truths—elements of this series—than happens in the interregnum. However, the period of the interregnum enables these series to be related to the idea itself as an infinity. "Commit to an Idea" also means that a long series of past events with the "touch of the absolute" opens up to us in a different way than it would in a situation when there is a presently existing truth. This principle is not a historically situated truth and its local consequences, but is an experimental rearrangement of elements in relation to the interregnum situation. In this rearrangement, we assume that all the elements of a long series are essentially equally near and far from us. Then in experimental rearrangements, the individual elements take positions according to what significance they have in relation to our situation in the interregnum.

I base this reasoning on Badiou's conception of historical connections that go against the flow of time. Badiou claims that in a certain respect, the emancipatory political and intellectual formations that arose in the 1840s are closer to our present situation than the ones that we are familiar with from the twentieth century. In the older era a radically emancipatory trend arose in the revolutionary wave of 1848, in the intellectual world there were Marx's manuscripts, and both of these formations faced the same question we are also facing. In the 1840s, capitalism was acting just as cynically as it does today. And it appeared then, just like it does now, that nothing else can exist. The main emancipatory question of that time was whether the idea of communism even exists, and if it does, how it can be theoretically and politically expressed. This is a question that we also face.[51] In the interregnum, there is a rearrangement of a long series of elements which participate in the infinity of the communist idea or are attributes of this absolute. Elements of the series, such as the "embryonic communist movement of 1848" and "Marx's manuscripts" are moved ahead of elements that were the embodiments of this idea in the twentieth century. Similarly, from the perspective of the interregnum, it's possible to rearrange a long series of elements connected with the idea of art. In the interregnum, elements that arose in a situation in which, like today, the artist struggled with the question of whether the idea of art even exists can come to the fore. These are, for example, works that appeared in the early Renaissance period, in a situation when the religious function of art had been exhausted and it wasn't clear whether art can have some other function. "Commit to an Idea" is a certain closure or completion of the postmodern approach to the past, in which the Enlightenment developmentalist conception of art and politics, according to which the closer a certain artwork or political form is to us, the more progressive this formation is, is disrupted. However, by contrast with the postmodern random combination of contemporary aesthetic and political elements with elements from previous periods, the rearrangements of long series are happening with the influence of the Idea. "Commit to an Idea" leads to an anticipation of new forms of its embedding. The rearrangement of long series of past events isn't led by the principle of play and randomness as it had been in postmodern culture, but it is realized because of future truths which are still unknown.

From *The Immanence of Truths* we can take the message that the interregnum is a period in which the task of philosophy is to interpret the world after the closing of truths, which has brought about a numbing domination of finiteness. Philosophy interprets the world of the interregnum as a first opening to the existence of infinity within it. As Badiou writes, the world of the interregnum gains a horizon against which our understanding of things changes. Our world is exposed to a measure of infinity. This is a measure of "the appearing of the finite in the realm of the infinite."[52] However, such a measure is paradoxical in nature because it compares the finite with the infinite, which eludes every scale of measurement. This measure means an excess. According to Badiou, human happiness consists in finding the right measure in variations of different logics, which can then be shared with a certain collective, with another person, or with oneself. "Happiness is actually the measure of excess [*la mesure de la démesure*], the measure of what we have not yet been able to measure in such a way that this measure is accepted everywhere."[53] Thus, we embrace an excessive measure of the immense by which the world of the interregnum is measured. "All happiness is a finite enjoyment of the infinite."[54] The task of philosophy is then to create the measure of the immense that is the source of happiness in the period of the interregnum.

Notes

Preface

1 Bauman, Z., Times of interregnum, *Ethics and Global Politics* 5, 2012, 1, pp. 49–56. Available at: https://www.tandfonline.com/doi/full/10.3402/egp.v5i1.17200/.

2 Graeber, D., *Debt. The First 5000 Years*, Melville, Brooklin – New York, 2011, p. 383.

3 Švihlíková, I., Tejkl, M., *Kapitalismus, socialismus a budoucnost aneb Mikeš už přišel*, [Capitalism, Socialism, and the Future, or *Mikeš Has Already Arrived]*, Rybka Publishers, Praha, 2017, p. 243.

4 Babic, M., Let's talk about the interregnum: Gramsci and the crisis of the liberal world order, *International Affairs* 96, 2020, 3, pp. 767–86. Available at: https://academic.oup.com/ia/article/96/3/767/5712430/.

5 Hauser, M., *Prolegomena k filosofii současnosti* [Prolegomena to a philosophy of our time*]*, Filosofia, Prague, 2007, p. 30.

6 Hauser, M., *Kapitalismus jako zombie neboli proč žijeme ve světě přízraků [Capitalism as a zombie, or why we live in a world of specters]*, Rybka Publishers, Praha, 2012, p. 7.

7 The meaning of this notion differs from the "transitory ontology" in Badiou's *Briefings on Existence* that expresses an "intervallic dimension" of his philosophy between the publication of *Being and Event* and *Logics of Worlds.* Badiou, A., *Briefings on Existence: A Short Treatise on Transitory Ontology*, State University of New York Press, New York, 2006, xi.

8 Badiou, A., *The Pornographic Age*, Bloomsbury, London – New York – Oxford, 2020, p. 19n.

9 Ibid., p. 20.

10 Badiou, A., *The Immanence of Truths. Being and Event III.*, Bloomsbury, London – New York – Oxford, 2022, p. 263.

11 Feinberg, J. G., Hauser, M., Ort, J., *Politika jednoty ve světě proměn* [The politics of unity in a world of changes], Filosofia, Praha, 2021.

Introduction

1 Jameson, F., *Postmodernism, or, The Cultural Logic of Late Capitalism*, Duke University Press, Durham, NC, 1991, p. x.

2 Ibid., p. 404.
3 Ibid., p. 416.
4 Ibid., p. 412.
5 Ibid., p. 407.
6 Badiou, A., *The Meaning of Sarkozy*, Verso, London – New York, 2008, p. 99.
7 Merleau-Ponty, M., *Humanism and Terror*, Beacon Press, Boston, 1969, p. 97.
8 Ibid., p. 179.
9 Courtois, S., Bartošek, K. et al., *The Black Book of Communism: Crimes, Terror, Repression*, Harvard University Press, Cambridge, MA, 1999; Perrault, G. et al., *Le Livre Noir du Capitalisme*, Le Temps des cerises, 1998.
10 Bondy, E., *Neuspořádaná samomluva* [Rambling Monologue], Luboš Marek, Brno, 2002, p. 65 nn.
11 Fukuyama, F., *The End of History and the Last Man*, Free Press, New York, 1992. Although Fukuyama's idea stems from Hegel's conception of political history, he does not base his understanding of liberal democracy on historical teleology. There is no guarantee based on historical laws that liberal-democratic principles will ultimately prevail. I understand Fukuyama as saying that if he does not acknowledge the (direct) influence of a historical teleology, he has to bring in another perspective, which is the question of whether these principles have historically been proven to work.
12 See Grimmes, W., *Eric J. Hobsbawm, Marxist Historian, Dies at 95* [online, accessed 18 January 2021]. Available at: https://www.nytimes.com/2012/10/02/arts/eric-hobsbawm-british-historian-dies-at-95.html?pagewanted=all&_r=0/.
13 Safi, M., Churchill´s policies contributed to the Bengal famine – study [online, accessed 26 October 2022]. Available at: https://www.theguardian.com/world/2019/mar/29/winston-churchill-policies-contributed-to-1943-bengal-famine-study.
14 Moyn, S., *The Last Utopia: Human Rights in History*, Harvard University Press, Cambridge, MA – London, 2010, p. 70.
15 Piketty, T., *Capital in the Twenty-First Century*, Harvard University Press, Cambridge, MA, 2014; Klein, N., *This Changes Everything: Capitalism vs. The Climate*, Simon & Schuster, New York, 2014.
16 There are many books that discuss the fatal concurrence of multiple crises of contemporary capitalism. For an overview, see Harvey, D., *Seventeen Contradictions and the End of Capitalism*, Oxford University Press, London, 2015.
17 Cílek, V., A composite crisis of the past and the situation today, in: Sušová-Salminen, V., Švihlíková, I. (eds.), *The Covid-19 Pandemic: The End of Neoliberal Globalization?* [online, accessed 24 January 2022]. Available at: http://casopisargument.cz/?p=33757
18 Hauser, M., The Covid-19 pandemic as a turning point. Why neoliberal capitalism is not a farce, but a tragedy, in: Sušová-Salminen, V., Švihlíková, I. (eds.), *The Covid-*

19 Pandemic: the End of Neoliberal Globalization? [online, accessed 24 January 2022]. Available at: http://casopisargument.cz/?p=33757

19 Schwab, K., Der Neoliberalismus hat ausgedient [online, accessed 24 January 2021]. Available at: https://www.zeit.de/wirtschaft/2020-09/corona-kapitalismus-rezession-wef-neoliberalismus-klaus-schwab?utm_referrer=https%3A%2F%2Fwww.google.cz%2F/.

20 Harvey, D., *Marx, Capital, and the Madness of Economic Reason*, Oxford University Press, New York, 2018, p. 72 nn.

21 I consider the concept of "cybersocialism" developed by Paul Cockshott and Allin Cottrell to be the most coherent proposal for a postcapitalist system. Their proposal is based on three elements: the labor theory of value, cybernetic planning, and participatory democracy, which offer an alternative to the liberal trio of price, market, and parliament. Cockshott, P. W., Cottrell, A., *Towards a New Socialism*, Spokesman, Nottingham, 1993. Available at: http://users.wfu.edu/cottrell/socialism_book/.

22 Fromm, E., *Marx´s Concept of Man*, Continuum, London – New York, 2004, p. 59.

23 Canfora, L., *Democracy in Europe: A History of an Ideology*, Blackwell Publishing, Oxford, 2006, p. 102.

24 Badiou, A., *Logics of Worlds*, Continuum, London – New York, 2009, p. 509. The "presence" means the presence of evental traces in a given world. See below for an explanation of this concept.

25 Bosteels, B., Translator's introduction, in: Badiou, A. (ed.), *Theory of the Subject*, Continuum, London – New York, 2009, p. xix.

26 Badiou, A., *The Meaning of Sarkozy*, p. 107.

27 Ibid., p. 113.

28 Ibid., p. 115.

29 Badiou, A., *The Pornographic Age*, p. 19 n.

30 Ibid., p. 20.

31 Dante Alighieri, *La Divina Commedia*, Inf. 1.16-18, trans. by Michael Hauser.

32 Althusser, L., *The Future Lasts Forever. A Memoir*, trans. R. Veasey, The New Press, New York, 1993, p. 111.

33 The term "generic procedure" and other concepts from Badiou's philosophy are explained in detail in the last part of the book. I usually use the concepts "generic procedure" and "truth procedure" as synonyms, even though the word "generic" has a more specific meaning than "truth." I explain this detail in the relevant part of the book.

34 Badiou, A., *Logics of Worlds*, p. 52.

35 Ibid., p. 49.

36 Ibid., p. 51.

37 Ibid., p. 52.

38 Ibid., p. 46.

39 Ibid., p. 27.

40 Ibid., p. 22.

41 Badiou, A., *The Communist Hypothesis*, Verso, London – New York, 2010, p. 250.

42 Ibid., p. 251.

43 Badiou, A., Third Sketch of a Manifesto of Affirmationist Art, in: Badiou, A. (ed.), *Polemics*, trans. S. Corcoran, Verso, London – New York, 2006, pp. 132–53.

44 Kužel, P., The Prague spring and the struggle for the workers' councils and self-governing socialism, in: Beránková, J. N., Hauser, M., Nesbitt, N. (eds.), *Revolutions for the Future: May'68 and Prague Spring*, Suture Press, Paris, 2020, p. 162 nn.

45 Badiou, A., *Logics of Worlds*, p. 60.

46 Based on a literary analysis of socialist realist novels, Vít Schmarc draws attention to a "sphere of a sphere defined by a higher order of existence, which rises above the world of mere shadows and reflections that are intended for ordinary mortals." With the help of mediators (Stalin) and "transit" holy sites (the Kremlin) it's possible to look into this sphere. Sometimes an immediate "touch of a higher principle" draws close. This especially happens at moments when physical light takes on a Leninist symbolic meaning and expresses the idea of progress. Schmarc, V., *Země lyr a ocele. Subjekty, ideologie, modely, mýty a rituály v kultuře českého stalinismu* [In The Land of Steel and Lyres: Subjects and Ideology in the Culture of Czech Stalinism (1948-1953)], Academia, Prague, 2017, p. 314.

47 Sartre, J.-P., Marxism and existentialism [online, accessed 28 January 2022]. Available at: https://www.marxists.org/reference/archive/sartre/works/critic/sartre1.htm.

48 Badiou, A., *The Immanence of Truths*, p. 568.

49 Goldman, W., *Terror and Democracy in the Age of Stalin*, Cambridge University Press, New York, 2007, p. 3.

50 Sartre, J.-P., Marxism and existentialism.

51 Ibid.

52 Canfora, L., *Democracy in Europe*, p. 216.

53 Adorno, Th. W., Marginalien zu Theorie und Praxis, in: ibid., *Gesammelte Schriften*, Vol. 10/2, Suhrkamp, Frankfurt am Main, 1977, p. 770 nn.

54 Badiou, A., *Logics of Worlds*, p. 61.

55 Badiou, A., *The Communist Hypothesis*, p. 54.

56 Ibid., p. 60.

57 Ibid., p. 56.

58 Ibid., p. 62.

59 Ibid., p. 102.

60 Ibid., p. 107.

61 Ibid., p. 277.

62 Ibid., p. 279. On the Cultural Revolution as a "political work," see *The Immanence of Truths*, p. 583 nn.

63 Tong, S., *Almost a Revolution*, Houghton Mifflin, Boston, 1990.

64 Calhoun, C., Revolution and repression in Tiananmen Square, *Society* 26, 1989, 6, pp. 21–38.

65 Badiou, A., *The Communist Hypothesis*, p. 35.

66 Skilling, G., *Czechoslovakia's Interrupted Revolution*, Princeton University Press, Princeton, 1976, p. 835.

67 Hauser, M., The emancipatory transfiguration of the state. Rancièrian politics and the Prague spring of 1968, in: Beránková, J. N., Hauser, M., Nesbitt, N. (eds.), *Revolutions for the Future: May '68 and Prague Spring*, p. 155.

68 Kober, J., Endeavoring another socialist law: Legal reformism in czechoslovakia and its significance, in: Beránková, J. N., Hauser, M., Nesbitt, N. (eds.), *Revolutions for the Future: May'68 and Prague Spring*, p. 208.

69 Badiou, A., *The Meaning of Sarkozy*, p. 111. "Political organization" came into being with Badiou's participation. He focuses his activities on providing aid for foreign workers and immigrants.

70 Krapfl, J., *Revolution with a Human Face: Politics, Culture, and Community in Czechoslovakia, 1989-1992*, Cornell University Press, Ithaca and London, 2013.

71 Derrida, J., *Specters of Marx*, Routledge, London – New York, 1994, p. 113.

72 Moyn, S., *The Last Utopia: Human Rights in History*.

73 Jameson, J., *Postmodernism*, p. 399.

Chapter 1

1 Whyte, J., *The Morals of the Market: Human Rights and the Rise of Neoliberalism*, Verso, London – New York, 2019, p. 17.

2 Ibid., p. 14.

3 Ibid., p. 19.

4 Ibid., p. 29.

5 Boltanski, L., Chiapello, E., *The New Spirit of Capitalism*, Verso, London – New York. 2005, p. 167 nn.

6 Ibid., p. 184.

7 Ibid., p. 188 n.

8 Ibid., p. 169.

9 Toms, M., *The Thatcher Privatization Legacy: Not Quite What She Planned?* [online, accessed 22 October 2020]. Available at: https://www.oxera.com/wp-content/uploads/2018/03/The-Thatcher-privatisation-legacy_1.pdf/.

10 Whyte, J., *The Morals of the Market*, p. 228.

11 Offe, C., *Contradictions of the Welfare State*, MIT Press, Cambridge, MA, 1984, p. 124. See also Hauser, M., Sociální stat a emancipační otázka [The welfare state and the question of emancipation], in: Hauser, M. (ed.), *Sociální stát a kapitalismus* [The welfare state and capitalism], Svoboda servis, SOK, Prague, 2007, p. 54 nn.

12 Foucault, M., *The Birth of Biopolitics. Lectures at the Collège de France, 1978–79*, trans. G. Burchell, Palgrave Macmillan, New York, 2008, p. 280.

13 In these lectures, Foucault speaks about American liberalism, which conceptually overlaps in his text with neoliberalism.

14 Ibid., p. 219

15 Ibid., p. 227 n.

16 Dean, M., The secret life of neoliberal subject, in: Schram, S. F., Pavlovskaya, M. (eds.), *Rethinking Neoliberalism: Resisting the Disciplinary Regime*, Routledge, London, 2018, p. 34.

17 Foucault, M., *The Birth of Biopolitics*, p. 259 n.

18 Dean, M., The secret life of neoliberal subject, p. 34.

19 Because of these statements, some authors speak of Foucault's inclination toward neoliberalism. Recently, see Zamora, D., *How Michel Foucault Got Neoliberalism So Wrong* [online, accessed 9 November 2021]. Available at: https://jacobinmag.com/2019/09/michel-foucault-neoliberalism-friedrich-hayek-milton-friedman-gary-becker-minoritarian-governments/.

20 Dean, M., *Governmentality: Power and Rule in Modern Society*, Sage, London, 2010, p. 73.

21 Lyotard, J.-F., *The Postmodern Explained. Correspondence 1982–1985*, trans. D. Barry et al., University of Minnesota Press, Minneapolis – London, 1993, p. 58.

22 Ibid., p. 59.

23 Foucault, M., *The Birth of Biopolitics*, p. 273.

24 Liessmann, K., *Theorie der Unbildung. Die Irrtümer der Wissensgesellschaft*, Zsolnay, Vienna, 2006.

25 Adorno, Th. W., Horkheimer, M., *Dialectic of Enlightenment*, trans. E. Jephcott, Stanford University Press, Stanford, CA, 2002, p. 136.

26 Adorno captured this transformation of human abilities into exchange value in his theory of cultural regression. The use value of art, through which artistic enjoyment has been connected with taste, changes into exchange value when works of art become cultural goods, which are evaluated according to unifying pseudoindividualistic categories such as liking or disliking. These categories are more fundamental in the perception of the work than the work itself. Art thus acquires a fetishistic character that corresponds to the fetishistic perception of its recipients. See Adorno, Th. W., Über den Fetischcharakter in der Musik und die Regression des Hörens, in: ibid., *Gesammelte Schriften*, Vol. 14, Suhrkamp, Frankfurt am Main, 1973, p. 22 nn.

27 Heilbrunn, J., *The Neoconservative Journey* [online, accessed 25 October 2020]. Available at: https://media.hoover.org/sites/default/files/documents/0817945725_105.pdf/.

Chapter 2

1 Derrida, J., *The Work of Mourning*, The University of Chicago Press, Chicago, 2001, p. 115.
2 Lyotard, J.-F., *The Postmodern Explained*, p. 78.
3 Jameson, F., *Postmodernism*, p. xv.
4 Huyssen, A., *After the Great Divide*, Indiana University Press, Bloomington, 1987, p. 168.
5 Hassan, I., *The Dismemberment of Orpheus*, The University of Wisconsin Press, London, 1982, p. 267 n.
6 Derrida, J., *Specters of Marx*, p. 28.
7 Toth, J., *The Passing of Postmodernism: A Spectroanalysis of the Contemporary*, Sunny Press, New York, 2010, p. 53.
8 Ibid., p. 56.
9 Ibid., p. 28.
10 Ibid., p. 29.
11 Hardt, M., Negri, A., *Multitude: War and Democracy in the Age of Empire*, Penguin Press, New York 2004, p. xv.
12 Huyssen, A., *After the Great Divide*, p. 193 n.
13 Jameson, F., *Postmodernism*, p. 275.
14 Huyssen, A., *After the Great Divide*, p. 194.
15 Huyssen, A., *After the Great Divide*, p. 196.
16 Toth, J., *The Passing of Postmodernism*, p. 14.

Introduction

1 Hauser, M., Dante's inferno and the contemporary situation of transition [Dantovo "Peklo" a současná situace přechodu], *Tvar* 30, 2019, 13, pp. 10–11.

Chapter 1

1 Brown, W., *Undoing the Demos: Neoliberalism's Stealth Revolution*, Zone Books, Cambridge, MA, 2015, p. 213. The author does not associate the demise of this

social contract with the extinction of the traces of communist elements because she does not relate her theory to a more general theory of the interregnum.

2 Ibid., p. 131.

3 Ibid., p. 132.

4 Ibid., p. 84.

5 Ibid., p. 216.

6 This contradiction between individualism and self-sacrifice was depicted satirically by Roman Sikora in the play *Confession of a Masochist* [Zpověď masochisty].

7 Adorno, Th. W., Horkheimer, M., *Dialectic of Enlightenment*, p. 42.

8 Brown, W., *Undoing the Demos*, p. 219.

9 Ibid., p. 84. Wendy Brown is only partially right because the neoliberal subject never had its own center if we consider that its center was an exchange relation. Brown notes in this context that Foucault's analysis of neoliberalism is insufficient on this point. Foucault was unaware that the neoliberal *Homo economicus* could arrive at the point of self-sacrifice.

10 Hauser, M., Populismus jako hlas Reálna. Ideologie sjednocení v éře radikální mnohosti [Populism as the voice of the Real. Ideological unification in the era of radical plurality], in: Takáč, P., Ruman, J. (eds.), *Slavoj Žižek a kritika ideológie* [Slavoj Žižek and the critique of ideology], OZ Pole, Košice, 2019, pp. 7–18.

11 Brown, W., *Undoing the Demos*, p. 71. Brown lacks a connection between the concept of the whole economy and "best practices," which implement the same approaches in different and separate areas of activity, and which represent their unifying link that creates the idea of something uniform in the diversity of individual economic and cultural fields.

12 Ibid., p. 136.

13 Jameson, F., *Postmodernism*, p. 120.

14 "Best practices" builds upon the "benchmarking" that was introduced in the 1970s. See Brown, W., *Undoing the Demos*, p. 136 nn.

15 Ibid., p. 136.

16 Liessmann, K., Liessmann, K., *Theorie der Unbildung.*

17 Agamben, G., *The Kingdom and the Glory: For a Theological Genealogy of Economy and Government*, Stanford University Press, Stanford, 2011, p. 281.

18 Badiou, A., *Second Manifesto for Philosophy*, Polity, Cambridge, p. 68 n.

19 Freud, S., *Beyond the Pleasure Principle*, trans. J. Strachey, W.W. Norton & Company, New York – London, 1975, p. 16.

Chapter 2

1 What was striking about the financial crisis in 2008 was that it was connected with a crisis of economic theory that had no ability to predict a financial crisis

even as a possibility, and which offered no conceptual tools to overcome its causes. See Hauser, M., Kapitalismus jako zombie neboli proč žijeme ve světě přízraků [*Capitalism as a zombie, or why we live in a world of specters*], p. 10 nn.

2 van den Akker, R., Gibbons, A., Vermeulen, T. (eds.), *Metamodernism: Historicity, Affect and Depth after Postmodernism*, Rowman & Littlefield, London – New York, 2017.

3 Rudrum, D., Stavris, N. (eds.), *Supplanting the Postmodern: An Anthology of Writings on the Arts and Culture of the Early 21st Century*, Bloomsbury, London – New York, 2015.

4 Critchley, S., *Theoretically Speaking* [online, accessed 2 April 2020]. Available at: https://www.frieze.com/article/theoretically-speaking/.

5 Eshelman, R., Performatism, or the end of postmodernism (*American Beauty*), in: Rudrum, D., Stavris, N. (eds.), *Supplanting the Postmodern*, p. 140.

6 Kirby, A., The death of postmodernism and beyond, in: Rudrum, D., Stavris, N. (eds.), *Supplanting the Postmodern*, p. 58.

7 Vermeulen, T., *Thirteen Theses on (the End of) Liberal Democracy* [online, accessed 2 April 2020]. Available at: http://www.metamodernism.com/2013/02/25/thirteen-theses-on-the-end-of-liberal-democracy/.

8 Critchley, S., *Theoretically Speaking*.

9 Badiou, A., *The Communist Hypothesis*, p. 37.

10 Žižek, S., Douzinas, K., Introduction, in: Žižek and Douzinas (eds.), *The Idea of Communism*, Verso, London – New York, 2010, p. ix.

11 Vattimo, G., Zabala, S., *Hermeneutic Communism: From Heidegger to Marx*, Columbia University Press, New York, 2011.

12 Žižek, S., *Pandemic! Covid-19 Shakes the World*, OR Books, London – New York, 2020.

13 Stavris, N., The anxieties of the present, in: Rudrum, D., Stavris, N. (eds.), *Supplanting the Postmodern*, p. 351.

14 Abbate, C., Parker, R., *A History of Opera. The Last Four Hundred Years*, Penguin Books, London, 2012, p. 63.

15 Vermeulen, T., van den Akker, Notes on metamodernism, in: Rudrum, D., Stavris, N. (eds.), *Supplanting the Postmodern*, p. 322.

16 Milbank, J., "Postmodern Critical Augustinianism": A short *Summa* in forty two responses to unasked questions, *Modern Theology* 7, 1991, 3, pp. 225–37.

17 Kirby, A., How new technologies dismantle the postmodern and reconfigure our culture, in: Rudrum, D., Stavris, N. (eds.), *Supplanting the Postmodern*, p. 280.

18 Ibid., p. 281.

19 Ibid., p. 282.

20 Ibid., p. 282 n.

21 Ibid., p. 283 nn.

22 For an overview article on the concept of the archipelago in contemporary philosophy and the social sciences, see Stratford, E. et al., Envisioning the Archipelago, *Island Studies Journal* 6, 2011, 2, pp. 113–30. Available at: https://ro .uow.edu.au/cgi/viewcontent.cgi?article=6404& context=scipapers/.
23 Bourriaud, N., Altermodern, in: Rudrum, D., Stavris, N. (eds.), *Supplanting the Postmodern*, p. 257.
24 McGowan, J., They might have been giants, in: Rudrum, D., Stavris, N. (eds.), *Supplanting the Postmodern*, p. 64.
25 Ibid., p. 68. Cf. McGowan, J., *Postmodernism and its Critics*, Cornell UP, Ithaca, NY, 1991, pp. 89–121.
26 McGowan, J., They Might Have Been Giants, p. 71.
27 Connor, S., Postmodernism grown old, in: Rudrum, D., Stavris, N. (eds.), *Supplanting the Postmodern*, p. 33 nn.
28 Hauser, M., *Cesty z postmodernismu* [Paths from Postmodernism], Filosofia, Praha, 2012, p. 17 nn.
29 Badiou, A., *Manifesto for Philosophy: Followed by Two Essays*, trans. N. Madarasz, State University of New York, Albany, 1999, p. 114.
30 Ibid., p. 116 n.
31 Ibid., p. 124.
32 Ibid., p. 84.
33 Nealon, J., Post-postmodernism: Or, the cultural logic of just-in-time capitalism, in: Rudrum, D., Stavris, N. (eds.), *Supplanting the Postmodern*, p. 94.
34 Lipovetsky, G., Time against time, or the hypermodern society, in: Rud-rum, D., Stavris, N. (eds.), *Supplanting the Postmodern*, p. 159.
35 Eshelman, R., "Introduction" *from* performatism, or the end of postmodernism, in: Rudrum, D., Stavris, N. (eds.), *Supplanting the Postmodern*, p. 114.
36 Stavris, N., The Anxieties of the Present, p. 350 n.
37 van den Akker, R., Vermeulen, T., Periodising the 2000s, or, the emergence of metamodernism, in: van den Akker, R., Gibbons, A., Vermeulen, T. (eds.), *Metamodernism*, p. 12.
38 Ibid., p. 8.
39 Ibid.
40 Hassan, I., Beyond postmodernism: Toward an aesthetic of trust, in: Rudrum, D., Stavris, N. (eds.), *Supplanting the Postmodern*, p. 13.
41 The name of a certain publishing house that publishes works from the "alt-right" is eloquent here: "Counter-Currents Publishing," and their motto is "Books against Time". Available at: https://www.counter-currents.com/.
42 The Generation Identity movement is understood either as a European part of the global alt-right movement, or as the European version of the American alt-right. Available at: https://www.ibtimes.co.uk/generation-identity-how-european-alt

-right-planning-british-invasion-1607986/ and also https://www.economist.com/europe/2016/11/12/meet-the-ib-europes-version-of-americas-alt-right/.

43 Defending "European identity"? The Dubious Struggle of Génération Identitaire [online, accessed 16 November 2020]. Available at: https://www.eyes-on-europe.eu/defending-european-identity-the-dubious-struggle-of-generation-identitaire/.

44 Willinger, M., *Generation Identity: A Declaration of War Against the ´68ers*, Arktos, London, 2013.

45 Sheehan, T., Myth and violence: The fascism of Julius Evola and Alain de Benoist, *Social Research* 48, 1981, 1, pp. 45–73. According to Sheehan de Benoist understands the organic state as an ideal that people should embrace and even potentially establish through violence.

46 Camus, J.-Y., Alain benoist and the new right, in: Sedgwick, M. (ed.) *The Key Thinkers of the Radical Right*, Oxford University Press, Oxford, 2019, p. 77.

47 De Benoist's essays are available at: https://www.telospress.com/now-available-alain-de-benoists-democracy-and-populism-the-telos-essays/.

48 Spektorowski, A., The new right: Ethno-regionalism, ethno-pluralism and the emergence of a neo-fascist 'Third Way', *Journal of Political Ideologies* 8, 2003, 1, p. 116.

49 Cf., for example, with communitarian proposals for democracy from below, which Christine Berry summarizes as the social vision of the new left. Berry, Ch., How the 21st century left thinks about economic democracy [online, accessed 29 January 2022]. Available at: https://www.ips-journal.eu/topics/democracy/how-the-21st-century-left-thinks-about-economic-democracy-4093/ . There is a significant intersection between these decentralizing proposals by the radical left and the ideas of part of the Identitarian movement.

50 De Benoist, A., *The Problem of Democracy*, Arktos, United Kingdom, 2011, p. 93.

51 Camus, J.-Y., Alain benoist and the new right, p. 77.

52 Spektorowski, A., The new right: Ethno-regionalism, ethno-pluralism and the emergence of a neo-fascist 'Third Way', p. 121 nn.

53 Ibid., p. 120.

54 Ibid., p. 117.

55 Camus, J.-Y., Alain benoist and the new right, p. 77.

56 Spektorowski, A., The new right: Ethno-regionalism, ethno-pluralism and the emergence of a neo-fascist 'Third Way', p. 126.

57 Ibid., p. 127.

58 Ibid., p. 118.

59 Hutcheon, L., *The Politics of Postmodernism*, Routledge, London – New York, 1989.

60 Flecha, R., de Botton, L., Santa Cruz, I., Claveria, J. V., Equality of differences versus postmodern racism, in: Macedo, D., Gounari, P. (eds.), *The Globalization of Racism*, Routledge, New York, 2006, p. 235.

61 De Benoist, A., *Beyond Human Rights: Defending Freedoms*, Arktos, United Kingdom, 2011, p. 63. He refers to de Maistre, Burke, Marx, and Arendt, who had criticized human rights for their abstract concept of the subject of these rights. Ibid., p. 81.

62 Lefebvre, A., Human rights in deleuze and Bergson's later philosophy, in: Sutter, L., McGee, K. (eds.), *Deleuze and Law*, Edinburgh University Press, Edinburgh, 2012, p. 50.

63 Ibid.

64 Christou, M., Not the same difference: How the new right hijacked an essential postmodern concept [online, accessed 16 November 2020]. Available at: https://www.radicalrightanalysis.com/2019/09/12/not-the-same-difference-how-the-new-right-hijacked-an-essential-postmodern-concept/.

65 In this point, Willinger differs from de Benoist, who had belonged to the radical right in 1968.

66 Badiou, A., *Logics of Worlds*, p. 54.

67 Moyn, S., *The Last Utopia*.

68 The postmodern left is characterized by its conception of identity as something established in a system of mutually-delimited differences, which is separate from any predetermined basis. De Benoist and part of the Identitarian movement also understand culture in the same way.

69 Vondrák, P., de Boëldieu, S., Proti internacionále obchodníků, za internacionálu národů! [Against an internationale of merchants, for an internationale of nations!] [online, accessed 16 November 2020]. Available at: https://deliandiver.org/2013/08/proti-internacionale-obchodniku-za-internacionalu-narodu.html/.

70 Vermeulen, T., van den Akker, R., Notes on metamodernism, p. 318.

71 Rudrum, D., Note on the supplanting of "Post-", in: Rudrum, D., Stavris, N. (eds.), *Supplanting the Postmodern*, p. 344.

72 Childish, B., Thomson, Ch., The stuckist manifesto, in: Rudrum, D., Stavris, N. (eds.), *Supplanting the Postmodern*, p. 104 nn.; Rudrum and Stavris (eds.), Remodernism, in: Ibid., p. 107 nn.

73 Available at: http://www.stuckism.com/. In the Czech Republic these impulses have been developed by Jiří Hauschka and Jaroslav Valečka. See also https://www.artlyst.com/features/stuckism-alive-well-living-prague-edward-lucie-smith/.

74 This citation and the ones above are in Artamonov, V. et al., Manifest radikálního realismu [Manifesto of Radical Realism] [online, accessed 16 November 2020]. Available at: https://artalk.cz/2016/09/06/manifest-radikalniho-realismu/.

75 Forman, D., Dopis k rozdílu mezi stuckismem a radikálním realismem [Letter on the Difference Between Stuckism and Radical Realism]. Source: the author's correspondence with Dominik Forman and Alexej Klyuykov.

76 Ibid.

77 Rudrum, D., Note on the supplanting of "Post-", p. 339 n.

78 Hassan, I., Beyond postmodernism: Toward an aesthetic of trust, p. 13.

79 Cf. with the figure of the radicalization of postmodernism as a starting point leading out of postmodernism that I have introduced in my other books. By contrast with Hassan, I conceive of the state of Nothingness or kenosis as a transit state and not a foundation. In my understanding, it is necessary to actively radicalize the state of Nothingness and kenosis by approaching real psychosomatic death. This experience of radicalized Nothingness establishes new standards or criteria for our relationship to the finite and the infinite. For more comparison of my conception of Nothingness with Hassan's, see below.

80 Jameson, F., *Postmodernism*, p. 95.

81 Eshelman, R., "Introduction" *from* performatism, or the end of postmodernism, p. 113 nn.

82 Eshelman, R., Performatism, or the end of postmodernism *(American Beauty)*, p. 123 n.

83 Jameson, F., *Postmodernism*, p. 10.

84 Gibbons, A., Metamodern affect, in: van den Akker, R., Gibbons, A., Vermeulen, T. (eds.), *Metamodernism*, p. 84.

85 Konstantinou, L., Four faces of postirony, in: van den Akker, R., Gibbons, A., Vermeulen, T. (eds.), *Metamodernism*, p. 97.

86 Milbank, J., "Postmodern Critical Augustinianism": A dhort *Summa* in forty two responses to unasked questions, p. 227.

87 Ibid., p. 234.

88 Heiser, J., Super-hybridity: Non-simultaneity, myth-making and multipolar conflict, in: van den Akker, R., Gibbons, A., Vermeulen, T. (eds.), *Metamodernism*, p. 58.

89 Ibid., p. 61.

90 Winter, Ch., *The Virtual "Caliphate": Understanding Islamic State's Propaganda Strategy*, London, Quilliam 2015. Available at: https://www.stratcomcoe.org/download/file/fid/2589/.

91 Hauser, M., Prasklá jednota liberální demokracie. K původu nových populismů [The fractured unity of liberal democracy: On the origin of new populisms], in: Feinberg, J. G., Hauser, M., Ort, J., *Politika jednoty ve světě proměn* [The politics of unity in a world of changes].

92 You can see representative selections in: van den Akker, R., Gibbons, A., Vermeulen, T. (eds.), *Metamodernism*. Also see this web page with examples of metamodernist art: http://www.metamodernism.com/.

93 Vermeulen, T., van den Akker, R., Misunderstandings and clarifications [online, accessed 16 November 2020]. Available at: http://www.metamodernism.com/2015/06/03/misunderstandings-and-clarifications/.

94 See, for example. Žižek, S., *The Ticklish Subject: The Absent Centre of Political Ontology*, Verso, London – New York, 2000, p. 250.
95 Hauser, M., Cesty z postmodernismu [*Paths from Postmodernism*], pp. 178–80.
96 Hauser, M., Cesty z postmodernismu [*Paths from Postmodernism*], p. 175 nn.; Za hranice postmodernismu [Beyond the boundaries of postmodernism], in: Kanda, R. (ed.), *Podzim postmodernismu. Teoretické výzvy současnosti* [Autumn of postmodernism. The present theoretical challenges], p. 258.
97 Hassan, I., Beyond postmodernism: Toward an aesthetic of trust, p. 26.
98 Konstantinou, L., Four faces of postirony, p. 93.
99 Toth, J., Brooks, N., Introduction: A wake and renewed?, in: Rudrum, D., Stavris, N. (eds.), *Supplanting the Postmodern*, p. 215.
100 Hassan, I., Beyond postmodernism: Toward an aesthetic of trust, p. 13.
101 Lipovetsky, G., Time against time, or the hypomodern society, p. 156 nn.
102 Badiou, A., *Logics of Worlds*, p. 54.
103 Ibid., p. 60.
104 Vermeulen, T., van den Akker, R., Utopia, Sort of: A case study in metamodernism, *Studia Neophilologica* 87, 2015, 1, pp. 55–67.
105 Hassan, I., Beyond postmodernism: Toward an aesthetic of trust, p. 14.
106 Žižek, S., Douzinas, K., Introduction, p. ix.

Introduction

1 Badiou, A., *The Immanence of Truths*, p. 86.
2 Badiou, A., *Being and Event*, p. 3.
3 Ibid.

Chapter 1

1 On the basis of an interpretation of Badiou's concepts, I have arrived at an answer to the question of which thesis is true in the subchapter "Badiou's philosophy as a ladder over the interregnum."
2 Badiou, A., *Manifesto for Philosophy*, p. 33.
3 Ibid., p. 34.
4 Ibid., p. 35.
5 Ibid., p. 62.
6 Ibid., p. 89.
7 Ibid.

8 I'm judging on the basis of two representative anthologies devoted to the relationship between Badiou's philosophy and truth procedures. See Riera, G. (ed.), *Alain Badiou: Philosophy and Its Conditions*, State University of New York Press, New York, 2005; Bowden, S., Duffy, p. (eds.), *Badiou and Philosophy*, Edinburgh University Press, Edinburgh, 2012. I attribute this oversight committed by Badiou's interpreters to the fact that in Badiou studies, the concept of the interval period (i.e., the present interregnum) has been considered marginal, and other types of questions were posed, and not the question of whether these truth procedures have not in reality already been closed, in conformity with Badiou's definition of the interval period.
9 Badiou, A., *Theory of the Subject*, p. 205.
10 Cf. Toscano, A., Marxism expatriated: Alain Badiou's turn, in: Bidet, J., Kouvelakis, S. (eds.), *Critical Companion to Contemporary Marxism*, Brill, Leiden – Boston, 2008, p. 544.
11 Ibid., p. 182.
12 Badiou, A., *Peut-on penser la politique?*, Seuil, Paris, 1985. Cited by Toscano, A., Marxism expatriated: Alain Badiou's turn, in: Bidet, J., Kouvelakis, S., *Critical Companion to Contemporary Marxism*, p. 536 n.
13 Ibid., p. 537.
14 Ibid., p. 538.
15 Nicolacopoulos, T., Vassilacopoulos, G., Philosophy and revolution: Badiou's infidelity to the event, in: Ashton, P., Bartlett, A. J., Clemens, J. (eds.), *The Praxis of Alain Badiou*, re.press, Melbourne, 2006, p. 377.
16 Badiou, A., *The Meaning of Sarkozy*, p. 113.
17 Ibid.
18 Ibid., p. 115.
19 Badiou, A., *The Communist Hypothesis*, p. 279.
20 Badiou, A., *The Meaning of Sarkozy*, p. 111. On "political organizations" see footnote above.
21 Badiou, A., *The Rebirth of History: Times of Riots and Uprisings*, Verso, London – New York, 2012, p. 5 n.
22 Ibid., p. 52.
23 Badiou, A., *Handbook of Inaesthetics*, Stanford University Press, Stanford, 2005, p. 15.
24 Badiou, A. Third sketch of a manifesto of affirmationist art, p. 134.
25 Ibid., p. 133 n.
26 Ibid., p. 133.
27 Badiou, A., Third sketch of a manifesto of affirmationist art, p. 142.
28 Ibid., p. 140
29 Ibid.

30 Ibid., p. 146.
31 Badiou, A., *The Immanence of Truths*, p. 501.
32 Badiou, A., *In Praise of Love*, Serpent's Tail, London, 2012. This is the motto of the entire book.
33 Ibid., p. 5 n.
34 Badiou, A., *The Meaning of Sarkozy*, p. 48.
35 Ibid.
36 Badiou, A., *The Pornographic Age*.
37 Ibid., p. 4; also see Badiou, *The Meaning of Sarkozy*, p. 91. Badiou makes it clear that he rejects the word democracy as a form of expressing depoliticized consensus but instead defends the positive meaning of the word as a government of the people. Badiou seeks to re-emancipate the appropriation of names such as democracy and communism. Unless it's necessary, he doesn't take the strategy of creating new names.
38 Badiou, A., *Logics of Worlds*, p. 2 n.
39 Badiou, A., *The Pornographic Age*, p. 5.
40 Ibid., p. 6.
41 Ibid., 4 n.
42 In Badiou's philosophy, *état* means the "state" or structure of the situation presented, but at the same time it also refers to "a state," which Badiou does not only consider a set of state institutions, but also a structure that gives formal status to their elements in a given society and defines the relationships between them.
43 Badiou, A., *In Praise of Love*, p. 29.
44 Ibid., p. 29.
45 Ibid., p. 25.
46 Ibid.
47 Ibid., p. 32.
48 Ibid., p. 90.
49 Ibid., p. 50.
50 Ibid., p. 56.
51 Badiou, A., *The Immanence of Truths*, p. 541.
52 Badiou, A., *In Praise of Love*, p. 28 n.
53 Badiou, A., Third sketch of a manifesto of affirmationist art, p. 134.
54 Ruda, F., *For Badiou: Idealism Without Idealism*, Northwestern University Press, Evanston, IL, 2015, p. 129.
55 Badiou, A., *Being and Event*, p. xii.
56 Ibid., p. 16.
57 Ibid., p. 13.
58 Ibid.
59 Ibid., p. 2.

60 Badiou introduced this term in the book *Theory of the Subject*. He coined it by combining the words "idealism" and Lacan's parodic neologism "linguisterie." Lacan connected the suffix "-erie," which has a pejorative meaning, to the word "linguistics." Bosteels, B., Translator's Introduction, in: Badiou, A., *The Theory of the Subject*, xxxiii. When he uses this term, Badiou is usually referring to an idea that has been widespread in part of Continental philosophy over the last few decades that it's necessary to conceive of all social, cultural, and psychological phenomena as a discourse.
61 Badiou, A., *Being and Event*, p. 46 n.
62 Badiou, A., *Logics of Worlds*, p. 538 n.
63 Badiou, A., *The Immanence of Truths*, p. 248.

Chapter 2

1 Badiou, A., *Being and Event*, p. 181.
2 See the third meditation in *Being and Event*, where Badiou represents the development of mathematical thinking that led to the emergence of contemporary set theory. The original goal of this mathematical development was to create a system in which Russell's paradox doesn't arise.
3 Badiou, A., *Being and Event*, p. 24.
4 Ibid., p. 26.
5 Ibid., p. 93 nn.
6 Ibid., p. 82 n.
7 Ibid., p. 175 n.
8 Ibid., p. 179.
9 I believe that Badiou's "structure of counting" (presentation and representation) is a concept compatible with Williams's "structure of feeling," which is applied in contemporary theories of the end of postmodernism. My hypothesis is that the "structure of feeling" is one of the concepts that is a mediating link between Badiou's philosophy and contemporary cultural theory—namely, metamodernist theory—which was discussed above. Badiou himself does not use this term.
10 Bensaïd, D., Alain Badiou and the miracle of the event, in: Hallward, P. (ed.), *Think Again: Alain Badiou and the Future of Philosophy*, Continuum, London – New York, 2004, p. 94 nn.
11 Badiou, A, *The Immanence of Truths*, p. 78 nn.
12 Badiou, A., *Being and Event*, p. 179.
13 Ibid., p. 181 nn.
14 Badiou, A., *Being and Event*, p. 207.
15 Ruda, F., *For Badiou: Idealism without Idealism*, p. 69.

16 Hauser, M., At the interface of contingency and history. Badiou´s concept of the event and historical materialism, *Paideia* 14, 2017, 1–2, pp. 1–7. [online, accessed 9 January 2022]. Available at: https://ojs.cuni.cz/paideia/article/view/1395/.

17 Badiou, A., *Being and Event*, p. 210.

18 Ibid., p. 206.

19 Ibid., p. 379.

20 Badiou, A., *Logics of Worlds*, p. 64.

21 Badiou, A., *Being and Event*, p. 233.

22 Ibid., p. 237.

23 Ibid., p. 234.

24 Ibid., p. 253. Badiou means mathematical procedures here. I interpret his triple determination of fidelity in a more general manner than it is done in Badiou's text.

25 Ibid., p. 391.

26 Ibid., p. 392.

27 Ibid., p. 394 n.

28 Ibid., p. 224.

29 Badiou relies on Gödel's incompleteness theorem, according to which there are theorems in every mathematical theory that are unprovable.

30 Badiou, A., *Being and Event*, p. 399.

31 Badiou, A., *Being and Event*, p. 401.

32 Ibid., p. 402.

33 Ibid.

34 Ibid., p. 396.

35 Feynman, R. P., The development of the time-space view of quantum electrodynamics (Nobel Lecture, December 11, 1965) [online, accessed 16 November 2020]. Available at: https://www.nobelprize.org/prizes/physics/1965/feynman/lecture/.

36 Schopenhauer, A., *The World as Will and Idea*, Vol. 2, trans. J. Kemp, Kegan Paul, Trench, Trübner & Co., London, 1909, p. 252.

37 Wittgenstein, L., *Tractatus logico-philosophicus*, trans. C. K. Ogden, Kegan, Paul, Trench, Trubner & Co., Ltd., London, 1922, p. 90.

Chapter 3

1 Badiou, A., *The Communist Hypothesis*, p. 229. Badiou distinguishes the writing of the word "idea" with a lowercase or uppercase first letter. The uppercase letter emphasizes that the idea is able to enter into human life as a transforming principle.

2 Badiou, A., *Second Manifesto for Philosophy*, Polity, Cambridge, 2011, p. 105 nn.

3 *The Immanence of Truths* was published in 2018. At the time when I wrote my book, Badiou's work had not yet been translated into English. In the scholarly literature, there were only a few fragmentary commentaries and no more detailed studies other than the one undertaken by Jana Beránková, which I write about below. This is why I don't refer to secondary literature in this chapter: it was still being written.
4 Badiou, A., *Sometimes, We Are Eternal*, p. 156.
5 Badiou, A., *The Immanence of Truths*, p. 43.
6 Ibid., p. 324.
7 Ibid., p. 327 nn.
8 Badiou, A., *Sometimes, We Are Eternal*, p. 151.
9 Beránková, J. N., The attributes of the absolute and Alain Badiou's response to Spinoza, in: Badiou, A., *Sometimes, We Are Eternal*, p. 176.
10 Badiou, A., *The Immanence of Truths*, p. 46.
11 Ibid., p. 341 n.
12 Ibid., p. 263.
13 Ibid., p. 262.
14 Ibid.
15 Ibid., p. 337.
16 A lemma is an ancillary statement that serves as an intermediate step in the proof of a more complex statement.
17 Badiou, A., *The Immanence of Truths,* p. 337.
18 Ibid., p. 342.
19 Ibid., p. 344.
20 Badiou does not work with the concept of the "downward directed set" as such, and he only concerns himself with certain of its aspects that are significant in his philosophy. I am mentioning this concept for the sake of completeness, and I'll decline to provide a general explanation because it isn't necessary for understanding Badiou's conception of the relationship between the absolute and truths.
21 Badiou, A., *The Immanence of Truths*, p. 345.
22 Ibid., p. 346.
23 Ibid., p. 348.
24 Ibid., p. 359.
25 Ibid., p. 361.
26 Ibid., p. 355.
27 Ibid., p. 362.
28 Ibid., p. 364.
29 Ibid., p. 465.
30 Ibid., p. 418.
31 Ibid., p. 419.
32 Ibid., p. 435.

33 Ibid., p. 234.

34 The interpretation of these very demanding theorems requires an explanation of a whole range of further concepts, such as the complete cardinal (Scott's Theorem) or the Ramsey cardinal. With regard to the subject of this chapter, I don't consider their explanation to be necessary here. In *The Immanence of Truths*, Badiou explains them on pp. 375nn. and 397 nn.

35 Badiou, A., *The Immanence of Truths*, p. 235.

36 Badiou, A., *Saint Paul: The Foundation of Universalism*, trans. R. Brassier, Stanford University Press, Stanford, CA, 2003, p. 1 n.

37 Badiou, A., *The Immanence of Truths*, p. 161.

38 Ibid., p. 75.

39 Ibid., p. 167.

40 Ibid., p. 168.

41 Ibid.

42 Tillich, P., *Theology of Culture*, Oxford University Press, London – Oxford – New York, 1964, p. 7.

43 Ibid., p. 61.

44 Ibid., p. 58.

45 Badiou, A., *The Immanence of Truths*, p. 235.

46 Ibid.

47 Badiou, A., *The Meaning of Sarkozy*, p. 117.

48 Badiou, A., *The Immanence of Truths*, p. 590.

49 Badiou, A., *Sometimes, We Are Eternal*, Suture, Lyon, 2019, p. 44.

50 Hauser, M., Za hranice postmodernismu [Beyond the boundaries of postmodernism], in: Kanda, R. (ed.), *Podzim postmodernismu. Teoretické výzvy současnosti* [Autumn of postmodernism. The present theoretical challenges], p. 272.

51 Badiou, A., *The Communist Hypothesis*, p. 259 n.

52 Badiou, A., *The Immanence of Truths*, p. 119.

53 Ibid.

54 Ibid.

Bibliography

Abbate, C., Parker, R., *A History of Opera. The Last Four Hundred Years*, Penguin Books, London 2012.

Adorno, Th. W., Über den Fetischcharakter in der Musik und die Regression des Hörens, in: idem, *Gesammelte Schriften*, Vol. 14, Suhrkamp, Frankfurt am Main 1973, pp. 14–50.

Adorno, Th. W., Marginalien zu Theorie und Praxis, in: *Gesammelte Schriften*, Vol. 10/2, Suhrkamp, Frankfurt am Main 1977, pp. 759–82.

Adorno, Th. W., Horkheimer, M., *Dialectic of Enlightenment*, trans. E. Jephcott, Stanford University Press, Stanford, California 2002.

Agamben, G., *The Kingdom and the Glory: For a Theological Genealogy of Economy and Government*, Stanford University Press, Stanford 2011.

Althusser, L., *The Future Lasts Forever. A Memoir*, trans. R. Veasey, The New Press, New York 1993.

Artamonov, V. et al., Manifest radikálního realismu [Manifesto of Radical Realism] [online, accessed 16 November 2020]. Available at: https://artalk.cz/2016/09/06/manifest-radikalniho-realismu/.

Babic, M., Let's talk about the interregnum: Gramsci and the crisis of the liberal world order, *International Affairs* 96, 2020, 3, pp. 767–86. Available at: https://academic.oup.com/ia/article/96/3/767/5712430/.

Badiou, A., *Peut-on penser la politique?*, Seuil, Paris 1985.

Badiou, A., *Manifesto for Philosophy: Followed by Two Essays*, trans. N. Madarasz, State University of New York, Albany 1999.

Badiou, A., *Saint Paul: The Foundation of Universalism*, trans. R. Brassier, Stanford University Press, Stanford, California 2003.

Badiou, A., *Handbook of Inaesthetics*, Stanford University Press, Stanford 2005.

Badiou, A., *Briefings on Existence: A Short Treatise on Transitory Ontology*, State University of New York Press, New York 2006.

Badiou, A., Third sketch of a manifesto of affirmationist art, in: Badiou, A. (ed.), *Polemics*, trans. S. Corcoran, Verso, London – New York 2006, pp. 132–53.

Badiou, A., *The Meaning of Sarkozy*, Verso, London – New York 2008.

Badiou, A., *Logics of Worlds, Being and Event II.*, Continuum, London – New York 2009.

Badiou, A., *Theory of the Subject*, Continuum, London – New York 2009.

Badiou, A., *The Communist Hypothesis*, Verso, London – New York 2010.

Badiou, A., *Second Manifesto for Philosophy*, Polity, Cambridge 2011.

Badiou, A., *In Praise of Love*, Serpent's Tail, London 2012.

Badiou, A., *The Rebirth of History: Times of Riots and Uprisings*, Verso, London – New York 2012.

Badiou, A., *Sometimes, We Are Eternal*, Suture, Lyon 2019.

Badiou, A., *The Pornographic Age*, Bloomsbury, London – New York – Oxford 2020.

Badiou, A., *The Immanence of Truths. Being and Event III.*, Bloomsbury, London – New York – Oxford 2022.

Bauman, Z., Times of interregnum, *Ethics and Global Politics* 5, 2012, 1, pp. 49–56. Available at: https://www.tandfonline.com/doi/full/10.3402/egp.v5i1.17200/.

Bensaïd, D., Alain Badiou and the miracle of the event, in: Hallward, P. (ed.), *Think Again: Alain Badiou and the Future of Philosophy*, Continuum, London – New York 2004, pp. 94–105.

Beránková, J. N., The attributes of the absolute and Alain Badiou's response to Spinoza, in: Badiou, A. (ed.), *Sometimes, We Are Eternal*, Suture, Lyon 2019, pp. 159–76.

Berry, Ch., How the 21st century left thinks about economic democracy [online, accessed 29 January 2022]. Available at: https://www.ips-journal.eu/topics/democracy/how-the-21st-century-left-thinks-about-economic-democracy-4093/.

Boltanski, L., Chiapello, E., *The New Spirit of Capitalism*, Verso, London – New York 2005.

Bondy, E., *Rambling Monologue* [Neuspořádaná samomluva], Luboš Marek, Brno 2002.

Bosteels, B., Translator's introduction, in: Badiou, A. (ed.), *Theory of the Subject*, Continuum, London – New York 2009, pp. vii–xxxvii.

Bourriuad, N., Altermodern, in: Rudrum, D., Stavris, N. (eds.), *Supplanting the Postmodern: An Anthology of Writings on the Arts and Culture of the Early 21st Century*, Bloomsbury, London – New York 2015, pp. 255–70.

Bowden, S., Duffy, S. (eds.), *Badiou and Philosophy*, Edinburgh University Press, Edinburgh 2012.

Brown, W., *Undoing the Demos: Neoliberalism's Stealth Revolution*, Zone Books, Cambridge, Mass., 2015.

Calhoun, C., Revolution and repression in Tiananmen square, *Society* 26, 1989, 6, pp. 21–38.

Camus, J.-Y., Alain Benoist and the new right, in: Sedgwick, M. (ed.), *The Key Thinkers of the Radical Right*, Oxford University Press, Oxford 2019, pp. 73–90.

Canfora, L., *Democracy in Europe: A History of an Ideology*, Blackwell Publishing, Oxford 2006.

Childish, B., Thomson, Ch., Remodernism, in: Rudrum, D., Stavris, N. (eds.), *Supplanting the Postmodern: An Anthology of Writings on the Arts and Culture of the Early 21st Century*, Bloomsbury, London – New York 2015, pp. 107–10.

Childish, B., Thomson, Ch., The stuckist manifesto, in: Rudrum, D., Stavris, N. (eds.), *Supplanting the Postmodern: An Anthology of Writings on the Arts and Culture of the Early 21st Century*, Bloomsbury, London – New York 2015, pp. 104–06.

Christou, M., Not the same difference: How the new right hijacked an essential postmodern concept [online: accessed 17 November 2020]. Available at: https://

www.radicalrightanalysis.com/2019/09/12/not-the-same-difference-how-the-new-right-hijacked-an-essential-postmodern-concept/.

Cílek, V., A composite crisis of the past and the situation today, in: Sušová-Salminen, V., Švihlíková, I. (eds.), *The Covid-19 Pandemic: The End of Neoliberal Globalization?* [online, accessed 24 January 2022]. Available at: http://casopisargument.cz/?p=33757.

Cockshott P. W., Cottrell, A., *Towards a New Socialism*, Spokesman, Nottingham 1993. Available at: http://users.wfu.edu/cottrell/socialism_book/.

Connor, S., Postmodernism grown old, in: Rudrum, D., Stavris, N. (eds.), *Supplanting the Postmodern: An Anthology of Writings on the Arts and Culture of the Early 21st Century*, Bloomsbury, London – New York 2015, pp. 31–48.

Courtois, S., Bartošek, K. et al., *The Black Book of Communism: Crimes, Terror, Repression*, Harvard University Press, Cambridge, Mass. 1999.

Critchley, S., *Theoretically Speaking* [online, accessed 2 April 2020]. Available at: https://www.frieze.com/article/theoretically-speaking.

Dante Alighieri, *Inferno*, trans. Mary Jo Bang, Graywolf Press, Minneapolis 2012.

De Benoist, A., *Beyond Human Rights: Defending Freedoms*, Arktos, United Kingdom 2011.

De Benoist, A., *The Problem of Democracy*, Arktos, United Kingdom 2011.

Dean, M., *Governmentality: Power and Rule in Modern Society*, Sage, London 2010.

Dean, M., The secret life of neoliberal subject, in: Schram, S. F., Pavlovskaya, M. (eds.), *Rethinking Neoliberalism: Resisting the Disciplinary Regime*, Routledge, London 2018, pp. 23–40.

Defending "European identity"? The Dubious Struggle of Génération Identitaire [online, accessed 16 November 2020]. Available at: https://www.eyes-on-europe.eu/defending-european-identity-the-dubious-struggle-of-generation-identitaire/.

Derrida, J., *Specters of Marx*, Routledge, London – New York 1994.

Derrida, J., *The Work of Mourning*, The University of Chicago Press, Chicago 2001.

Eshelman, R., "Introduction" *from* performatism, or the end of postmodernism, in: Rudrum, D., Stavris, N. (eds.), *Supplanting the Postmodern: An Anthology of Writings on the Arts and Culture of the Early 21st Century*, Bloomsbury, London – New York 2015, pp. 113–16.

Eshelman, R., Performatism, or the end of postmodernism (*American Beauty*), in: Rudrum, D., Stavris, N. (eds.), *Supplanting the Postmodern: An Anthology of Writings on the Arts and Culture of the Early 21st Century*, Bloomsbury, London – New York 2015, pp. 117–52.

Feinberg, J. G., Hauser, M., Ort, J., *Politika jednoty ve světě proměn* [The politics of unity in a world of changes], Filosofia, Praha 2021.

Feynman, R. P., The development of the time-space view of quantum electrodynamics (Nobel Lecture, December 11, 1965) [online, accessed 16 November 2020]. Available at: https://www.nobelprize.org/prizes/physics/1965/feynman/lecture/.

Flecha, R., de Botton, L., Santa Cruz, I., Claveria, J. V., Equality of differences versus postmodern racism, in: Macedo, D., Gounari, P. (eds.), *The Globalization of Racism*, Routledge, New York 2006, pp. 223–40.

Forman, D., Dopis k rozdílu mezi stuckismem a radikálním realismem [Letter on the difference between Stuckism and Radical Realism]. Source: the author's correspondence with Dominik Forman and Alexej Klyuykov.

Foucault, M., *The Birth of Biopolitics. Lectures at the Collège de France, 1978–79*, trans. G. Burchell, Palgrave Macmillan, New York 2008.

Freud, S., *Beyond the Pleasure Principle*, trans. J. Strachey, W.W. Norton & Company, New York - London 1975.

Fromm, E., *Marx´s Concept of Man*, Continuum, London - New York 2004, p. 59.

Fukuyama, F., *The End of History and the Last Man*, Free Press, New York 1992.

Gibbons, A., Metamodern affect, in: Van den Akker, R., Gibbons, A., Vermeulen, T. (eds.), *Metamodernism: Historicity, Affect and Depth After Postmodernism*, Rowman and Littlefield, London - New York 2017, pp. 83–6.

Goldman, W., *Terror and Democracy in the Age of Stalin*, Cambridge University Press, New York 2007.

Graeber, D., *Debt. The First 5000 Years*, Melville, Brooklin - New York 2011.

Grimmes, W., *Eric J. Hobsbawm, Marxist Historian, Dies at 95.* Available at: https://www.nytimes.com/2012/10/02/arts/eric-hobsbawm-british-historian-dies-at-95.html?pagewanted=all&_r=0/.

Hardt, M., Negri, A., *Multitude: War and Democracy in the Age of Empire*, Penguin Press, New York 2004,

Harvey, D., *Seventeen Contradictions and the End of Capitalism*, Oxford University Press, London 2015.

Harvey, D., *Marx, Capital, and the Madness of Economic Reason*, Oxford University Press, New York 2018.

Hassan, I., Beyond postmodernism: Toward an aesthetic of trust, in: Rudrum, D., Stavris, N. (eds.), *Supplanting the Postmodern: An Anthology of Writings on the Arts and Culture of the Early 21st Century*, Bloomsbury, London - New York 2015, pp. 13–30.

Hassan, I., *The Dismemberment of Orpheus*, The University of Wisconsin Press, London 1982.

Hauser, M., *Prolegomena k filosofii současnosti* [Prolegomena to a philosophy of our time], Filosofia, Praha 2007.

Hauser, M., Sociální stát a emancipační otázka [The welfare state and the question of emancipation], in: Hauser, M. (ed.), *Sociální stát a kapitalismus* [The welfare state and capitalism], Svoboda servis, SOK, Praha 2007, pp. 16–77.

Hauser, M., *Cesty z postmodernismu* [Paths from Postmodernism], Filosofia, Praha 2012.

Hauser, M., *Kapitalismus jako zombie neboli proč žijeme ve světě přízraků* [Capitalism as a zombie, or why we live in a world of specters], Rybka Publishers, Praha 2012.

Hauser, M., Za hranice postmodernismu [Beyond the boundaries of postmodernism], in: Kanda, R. (ed.), *Podzim postmodernismu. Teoretické výzvy současnosti* [Autumn of postmodernism. The present theoretical challenges], Filosofia, Prague 2016, pp. 223–86.

Hauser, M., At the interface of contingency and history. Badiou´s concept of the event and historical materialism, *Paideia* 14, 2017, 1–2, pp. 1–7. Available at: https://ojs.cuni.cz/paideia/article/view/1395/.

Hauser, M., Dante's "Inferno" and the contemporary situation of transition [Dantovo "Peklo" a současná situace přechodu], *Tvar* 30, 2019, 13, pp. 10–11.

Hauser, M., Populismus jako hlas Reálna. Ideologie sjednocení v éře radikální mnohosti [Populism as the voice of the Real. Ideological unification in the era of radical plurality], in: Takáč, P., Ruman, J. (eds.), *Slavoj Žižek a kritika ideológie* [Slavoj Žižek and the critique of ideology], OZ Pole, Košice 2019, pp. 7–18.

Hauser, M., The emancipatory transfiguration of the state. Rancièrian politics and the Prague spring of 1968, in: Berankova, J. N., Hauser, M., Nesbitt, N. (eds.), *Revolutions for the Future: May'68 and Prague Spring*, Suture Press, Paris 2020, pp. 140–61.

Hauser, M., The Covid-19 pandemic as a turning point. Why neoliberal capitalism is not a farce, but a tragedy, in: Sušová-Salminen, V., Švihlíková, I. (eds.), *The Covid-19 Pandemic: The End of Neoliberal Globalization?* [online, accessed 24 January 2022]. Available at: http://casopisargument.cz/?p=33757.

Hauser, M., Prasklá jednota liberální demokracie. K původu nových populismů [The fractured unity of liberal democracy: On the origin of new populisms], in: Feinberg, J. G., Hauser, M., Ort, J. (eds.), *Politika jednoty ve světě proměn* [The politics of unity in a world of changes], Filosofia, Praha 2021, pp. 95–169.

Heilbrunn, J., *The Neoconservative Journey* [online, accessed 25 October 2020]. Available at: https://media.hoover.org/sites/default/files/documents/0817945725_105.pdf/.

Heiser, J., Super-Hybridity: Non-simultaneity, myth-making and multipolar conflict, in: Van den Akker, R., Gibbons, A., Vermeulen, T. (eds.), *Metamodernism: Historicity, Affect and Depth After Postmodernism*, Rowman and Littlefield, London – New York 2017, pp. 55–68.

Hutcheon, L., *The Politics of Postmodernism*, Routledge, London – New York 1989.

Huyssen, A., *After the Great Divide*, Indiana University Press, Bloomington 1987.

Jameson, F., *Postmodernism, or, The Cultural Logic of Late Capitalism*, Duke University Press, Durham, NC. 1991.

Kirby, A., The death of postmodernism and beyond, in: Rudrum, D., Stavris, N. (eds.), *Supplanting the Postmodern: An Anthology of Writings on the Arts and Culture of the Early 21st Century*, Bloomsbury, London – New York 2015, pp. 49–60.

Kirby, A., How new technologies dismantle the postmodern and reconfigure our culture, in: Rudrum, D., Stavris, N. (eds.), *Supplanting the Postmodern: An Anthology of Writings on the Arts and Culture of the Early 21st Century*, Bloomsbury, London – New York 2015, pp. 273–304.

Klein, N., *This Changes Everything: Capitalism vs. The Climate*, Simon & Schuster, New York 2014.

Kober, J., Endeavoring another socialist law: Legal reformism in Czechoslovakia and its significance, in: Berankova, J. N., Hauser, M., Nesbitt, N. (eds.), *Revolutions for the Future: May'68 and Prague Spring*, Suture Press, Paris 2020, pp. 196–215.

Konstantinou, L., Four faces of postirony, in: Van den Akker, R., Gibbons, A., Vermeulen, T. (eds.), *Metamodernism: Historicity, Affect and Depth After Postmodernism*, Rowman and Littlefield, London – New York 2017, pp. 87–116.

Krapfl, J., *Revolution with a Human Face: Politics, Culture, and Community in Czechoslovakia, 1989–1992*, Cornell University Press, Ithaca and London 2013.

Kužel, P., The prague spring and the struggle for the worker's councils and self-governing socialism, in: Berankova, J. N., Hauser, M., Nesbitt, N. (eds.), *Revolutions for the Future: May '68 and Prague Spring*, Suture Press, Paris 2020, pp. 162–95.

Lefebvre, A., Human rights in Deleuze and Bergson´s later philosophy, in: Sutter, L., McGee, K. (eds.), *Deleuze and Law*, Edinburgh University Press, Edinburgh 2012, pp. 48–68.

Liessmann, K., *Theorie der Unbildung. Die Irrtümer der Wissensgesellschaft*, Zsolnay, Vienna 2006.

Lipovetsky, G., Time against time, or the hypermodern society, in: Rudrum, D., Stavris, N. (eds.), *Supplanting the Postmodern: An Anthology of Writings on the Arts and Culture of the Early 21st Century*, Bloomsbury, London – New York 2015, pp. 156–72.

Lyotard, J.-F., *The Postmodern Explained. Correspondence 1982–1985*, trans. D. Barry et al., University of Minnesota Press, Minneapolis – London 1993.

McGowan, J., *Postmodernism and its Critics*, Cornell University Press, Ithaca, NY, 1991.

McGowan, J., They might have been giants, in: Rudrum, D., Stavris, N. (eds.), *Supplanting the Postmodern: An Anthology of Writings on the Arts and Culture of the Early 21st Century*, Bloomsbury, London – New York 2015, pp. 61–74.

Merleau-Ponty, M., *Humanism and Terror*, Beacon Press, Boston 1969.

Milbank, J., "Postmodern critical augustinianism": A short *summa* in forty two responses to unasked questions, *Modern Theology* 7, 1991, 3, pp. 225–37.

Moyn, S., *The Last Utopia: Human Rights in History*, Harvard University Press, Cambridge, Mass., London 2010.

Nealon, J., Post-postmodernism: Or, the cultural logic of just-in-time capitalism, in: Rudrum, D., Stavris, N. (eds.), *Supplanting the Postmodern: An Anthology of Writings on the Arts and Culture of the Early 21st Century*, Bloomsbury, London – New York 2015, pp. 75–98.

Nicolacopoulos, T., Vassilacopoulos, G., Philosophy and revolution: Badiou's infidelity to the event, in: Ashton, P., Bartlett, A. J., Clemens, J. (eds.), *The Praxis of Alain Badiou*, re.press, Melbourne 2006, pp. 367–86.

Offe, C., *Contradictions of the Welfare State*, MIT Press, Cambridge, Mass., 1984.

Perrault, G. et al., *Le Livre Noir du Capitalisme*, Le Temps des cerises 1998.

Piketty, T., *Capital in the Twenty-First Century*, Harvard University Press, Cambridge, Mass. 2014.

Riera, G. (ed.), *Alain Badiou: Philosophy and Its Conditions*, State University of New York Press, New York 2005.

Ruda, F., *For Badiou: Idealism Without Idealism*, Northwestern University Press, Evanston, Ill., 2015.

Rudrum, D., Note on the supplanting of "Post-", in: Rudrum, D., Stavris, N. (eds.), *Supplanting the Postmodern: An Anthology of Writings on the Arts and Culture of the Early 21st Century*, Bloomsbury, London – New York 2015, pp. 333–48.

Rudrum, D., Stavris, N. (eds.), *Supplanting the Postmodern: An Anthology of Writings on the Arts and Culture of the Early 21st Century*, Bloomsbury, London – New York 2015.

Safi, M., Churchill´s policies contributed to Bengal famine – study [online, accessed 26 October 2022]. Available at: https://www.theguardian.com/world/2019/mar/29/winston-churchill-policies-contributed-to-1943-bengal-famine-study.

Sartre, J.-P., Marxism and existentialism [online, accessed 28 January 2022]. Available at: https://www.marxists.org/reference/archive/sartre/works/critic/sartre1.htm.

Sheehan, T., Myth and violence: The fascism of Julius Evola and Alain de Benoist, *Social Research* 48, 1981, 1, pp. 45–73.

Schmarc, V., *In The Land of Steel and Lyres: Subjects and Ideology in the Culture of Czech Stalinism (1948–1953)* [Země lyr a ocele. Subjekty, ideologie, modely, mýty a rituály v kultuře českého stalinismu], Academia, Prague 2017.

Schopenhauer, A., *The World as Will and Idea*, Vol. 2, trans. J. Kemp, Kegan Paul, Trench, Trübner & Co., London 1909.

Schwab, K., "Der Neoliberalismus hat ausgedient" [online, accessed 24 January 2021]. Available at: https://www.zeit.de/wirtschaft/2020-09/corona-kapitalismus-rezession-wef-neoliberalismus-klaus-schwab?utm_referrer=https%3A%2F%2Fwww.google.cz%2F/.

Skilling, G., *Czechoslovakia's Interrupted Revolution*, Princeton University Press, Princeton 1976.

Spektorowski, A., The new right: Ethno-regionalism, ethno-pluralism and the emergence of a neo-fascist 'Third Way', *Journal of Political Ideologies* 8, 2003, 1, pp. 111–30.

Stavris, N., The anxieties of the present, in: Rudrum, D., Stavris, N. (eds.), *Supplanting the Postmodern: An Anthology of Writings on the Arts and Culture of the Early 21st Century*, Bloomsbury, London – New York 2015, pp. 349–64.

Stratford, E. et al., Envisioning the archipelago, *Island Studies Journal* 6, 2011, 2, pp. 113–30. Available at: https://ro.uow.edu.au/cgi/viewcontent.cgi?article=6404&context=scipapers/.

Švihlíková, I., Tejkl, M., *Kapitalismus, socialismus a budoucnost aneb Mikeš už přišel* [Capitalism, Socialism, and the Future, or *Mikeš Has Already Arrived*], Rybka Publishers, Praha 2017.

Tillich, P., *Theology of Culture*, Oxford University Press, London – Oxford – New York 1964.

Toms, M., *The Thatcher Privatization Legacy: Not Quite What She Planned?* [online, accessed 22 October 2020]. Available at: https://www.oxera.com/wp-content/uploads/2018/03/The-Thatcher-privatisation-legacy_1.pdf/.

Tong, S., *Almost a Revolution*, Houghton Mifflin, Boston 1990.

Toscano, A., Marxism expatriated: Alain Badiou's turn, in: Bidet, J., Kouvelakis, S. (eds.), *Critical Companion to Contemporary Marxism*, Brill, Leiden – Boston 2008, pp. 529–48.

Toth, J., *The Passing of Postmodernism: A Spectroanalysis of the Contemporary*, Sunny Press, New York 2010.

Toth, J., Brooks, N., Introduction: A wake and renewed?, in: Rudrum, D., Stavris, N. (eds.), *Supplanting the Postmodern: An Anthology of Writings on the Arts and Culture of the Early 21st Century*, Bloomsbury, London – New York 2015, pp. 209–18.

Van den Akker, R., Vermeulen, T., Periodisining the 2000s, or, the emergence of metamodernism, in: Van den Akker, R., Gibbons, A., Vermeulen, T. (eds.), *Metamodernism: Historicity, Affect and Depth After Postmodernism*, Rowman and Littlefield, London – New York 2017, pp. 1–20.

Van den Akker, R., Gibbons, A., Vermeulen, T. (eds.), *Metamodernism: Historicity, Affect and Depth after Postmodernism*, Rowman & Littlefield, London – New York 2017.

Vattimo, G., Zabala, S., *Hermeneutic Communism: From Heidegger to Marx*, Columbia University Press, New York 2011.

Vermeulen, T., *Thirteen Theses on (the End of) Liberal Democracy* [online, accessed 2 April 2020]. Available at: http://www.metamodernism.com/2013/02/25/thirteen-theses-on-the-end-of-liberal-democracy/.

Vermeulen, T., van den Akker, Notes on metamodernism, in: Rudrum, D., Stavris, N. (eds.), *Supplanting the Postmodern: An Anthology of Writings on the Arts and Culture of the Early 21st Century*, Bloomsbury, London – New York 2015, pp. 309–20.

Vermeulen, T., van den Akker, R., Utopia, Sort of: A case study in metamodernism, *Studia Neophilologica* 87, 2015, 1, pp. 55–67.

Vermeulen, T., van den Akker, R., *Misunderstandings and Clarifications* [online, accessed 16 November 2020]. Available at: http://www.metamodernism.com/2015/06/03/misunderstandings-and-clarifications/.

Vondrák, P., de Boëldieu, S., Against an internationale of merchants, for an internationale of nations! [Proti internacionále obchodníků, za internacionálu národů!] [online, accessed 16 November 2020]. Available at: https://deliandiver.org/2013/08/proti-internacionale-obchodniku-za-internacionalu-narodu.html/.

Whyte, J., *The Morals of the Market: Human Rights and the Rise of Neoliberalism*, Verso, London – New York 2019.

Willinger, M., *Generation Identity: A Declaration of War Against the '68ers*, Arktos, London 2013.

Winter, Ch., *The Virtual "Caliphate": Understanding Islamic State's Propaganda Strategy*, London, Quilliam 2015. Available at: https://www.stratcomcoe.org/download/file/fid/2589/.

Wittgenstein, L., *Tractatus logico-philosophicus*, trans. C. K. Ogden, Kegan, Paul, Trench, Trubner & Co., Ltd., London 1922.

Zamora, D., *How Michel Foucault Got Neoliberalism So Wrong* [online, accessed 9 November 2021]. Available at: https://jacobinmag.com/2019/09/michel-foucault-neoliberalism-friedrich-hayek-milton-friedman-gary-becker-minoritarian-governments/.

Žižek, S., *The Ticklish Subject. The Absent Centre of Political Ontology*, Verso, London – New York 2000.

Žižek, S., *Pandemic! Covid-19 Shakes the World*, OR Books, London – New York 2020.

Žižek, S., Douzinas, K., Introduction, in: Žižek and Douzinas (eds.), *The Idea of Communism*, Verso, London – New York 2010, pp. vii–x.

Other internet sources:

https://www.telospress.com/now-available-alain-de-benoists-democracy-and-populism-the-telos-essays/.

https://artalk.cz/2016/09/06/manifest-radikalniho-realismu/.

http://www.metamodernism.com/.

http://www.stuckism.com/.

https://www.artlyst.com/features/stuckism-alive-well-living-prague-edward-lucie-smith/.

https://www.ibtimes.co.uk/generation-identity-how-european-alt-right-planning-british-invasion-1607986/.

https://www.economist.com/europe/2016/11/12/meet-the-ib-europes-version-of-americas-alt-right/.

https://www.counter-currents.com/.

Index

Note: Page numbers in *italics* refer to figures. Page numbers followed by "n" refer to notes

www.ingramcontent.com/pod-product-compliance
Ingram Content Group UK Ltd.
Pitfield, Milton Keynes, MK11 3LW, UK
UKHW020240290926
15470UKWH00002B/643

9 781350 437845